a realistic perspective about their development: *"The stubbornness of my belief disavowed any hostile coexistence between expectation and reality. As in every child's mind, expectation trumps everything. I wanted to be first in the class and expected to be."*

As an adult, he faced engineering challenges, war zones, and political and social strife; but the overriding lessons learned early about the importance of kindness and aspirations remained stalwart against all obstacles. They come full circle in the story of how a moment of childhood revelation about bringing light to a dark classroom translates into adult achievements during a terrible war.

Readers looking for memoirs that offer insights into Nigerian community and culture and a young boy's process of actualizing what seems like an impossible dream will find *The Courage To Aspire* an inspirational blend of spiritual and psychological accomplishment that documents the rocky road to triumph and success.

—The Midwest Review

✻ ✻ ✻

We have resolved each reviewer's issues through final editing and made this book truly enjoyable.

The
Courage
To
Aspire

Thoughts On Moments Of Love, Kindness, Encouragement, And Aspiration

Chuks I. Ndukwe

What Reviewers Wrote About The Courage To Aspire

The Courage to Aspire is certainly an eye-opening coming of age memoir. Our narrator takes the reader on a shared pilgrimage of exposing the true power of human kindness. It champions the importance of receiving an education and perpetuating those values in one's current life. And educates the reader on Nigerian culture and leaves us on an axis of realization. "As the plane began to taxi to the takeoff point, my faith and belief in the infinite goodness and mercy of God—even for the undeserving like me--grew stronger."

—Independent Book Review

What strikes me reading this inspiring memoir apart from his achievements is that the author is a sweet young man to follow around; so I did. Chuks loves his family especially his parents, Uncles, and his cousin Egbichi. He loves school and his teachers especially Mr. and Mrs. Okocha and they love him too. It is not surprising; he is simply lovable.

Some parts are amusing and I could not stop smiling as I read his reaction when his mother picked him up for coming third in his examination; struggling to express his manhood, he tells his mother, "Maa, I am not a baby. Let me go; other kids will see us." We all share that embarrassment as we grow away from our parents. We've all been there and know the feeling.

Another thing that is pleasantly unique about this memoir is how Chuks captured his magic moment while assisting an American scientists who conducted technical demonstrations in his class. That moment lit up his imagination to aspire to become what he ended up becoming with the help of his teacher who noticed his burning desire and made it happen. I enjoyed reading this book and find it inspiring.

—Nadine, ARC Reviewer

The Courage to Aspire starts by declaring "it is during our growing days that the magic happens—when the inspired mind awakens the inner-power to lead the way and invites hope, courage, and aspiration to fulfil its purpose." Without a doubt the author's growing days was indeed his wonder years during which he awakened his inner-power to lead him out of economic challenges.

It is heartwarming to follow the young Chuks I. Ndukwe around to church, school, and his teachers' homes where he enjoyed moments of love, kindness, and encouragement.

This narrative is not only inspirational, but it also captures the essence of the author's lovable gentle nature. I wish his mother had lived to see the product of her nine-month making of a sweet loving man.

—Samantha, ARC Review

The Courage To Aspire: Thoughts On Moments Of Love, Kindness, Encouragement, And Aspiration is a memoir of how a young African village boy with limited financial resources crafted some big dreams of becoming an electrical engineer and succeeded in making them come true, absorbing some valuable life lessons in the process. It opens with the reflection of how life is a journey into hope and fulfillment, moves into the 'wonder years' of childhood, and examines village experiences through the lens of nostalgia, detailing the roots of inspiration and the even more important discovery that *"...inspiration alone is not sufficient; it has to be accompanied by hope, courage, and aspiration to become real."*

As readers follow Chuks I. Ndukwe through his childhood play, village encounters and culture, and life lessons about facing conflict and developing realistic goals, they receive insights into the cultural and religious influences that helped drive his goals and also led him to hone

The Courage To Aspire:
Thoughts On Moments Of Love, Kindness, Encouragement, And Aspiration

Copyright © 2018 by Chuks I. Ndukwe
All Rights Reserved.
Published by: Ikebiebooks in association with Ingram Sparks: Distributed by Ingram.

This publication may not be reproduced in whole or in part. It may not be transmitted in any form or means, electronic or mechanical, or stored in a retrieval system.

Publisher's Cataloging-In-Publication Data
(Prepared by The Donohue Group, Inc.)

Names: Ndukwe, Chuks I., 1942-
Title: The courage to aspire: thoughts on moments of inspiration, love, kindness, hope, and courage / Chuks I. Ndukwe.
Description: [Newark, New Jersey] : Ikebiebooks, [2018]
Identifiers: ISBN 9780999070550 (paperback) | ISBN 099907055X (paperback) | ISBN 9780999070567 (ebook) | ISBN 0999070568 (ebook)
Subjects: LCSH: Ndukwe, Chuks I., 1942- | Self-actualization (Psychology) | Courage. | Electrical engineers--Nigeria--Psychology.
Classification: LCC BF637.S4 N38 2018 (print) | LCC BF637.S4: LCCN: 2018907546

info@ikebiebooks.com
855-336-7770

Dedication

To those who aspire to reach their goal.

Contents

Epigraph x
Prologue xi
    Chapter 1 1
Peer Applause..1
    Chapter 2 12
First Step Forward...12
    Chapter 3 23
Leaving Home..23
    Chapter 4 33
A Lesson in Reality...33
    Chapter 5 43
Fear Of failure..43
    Chapter 6 57
Sweet Reunion 57
    Chapter 7 68
The Best Christmas Ever...68
    Chapter 8 77
A Moment Of Inspiration...77
    Chapter 9 90
Short Visit Abroad 90
    Chapter 10 100
Encouragement and Aspiration..................................100
    Chapter 11 112
Spiritual Enrichment 112
    Chapter 12 127
Second Step Forward 127
    Chapter 13 137
The Wrong Way To Start..137
    Chapter 14 154

The Courage To Aspire

Biafra-Nigeria War 154
    Chapter 15 163
Fitting Reward 163
    Chapter 16 170
Giving Back 170
Epilogue 186
Acknowledgements 190
Glossary of Igbo Words 191
About The Author 194

Epigraph

***

Life is a journey that starts from the day we are born and takes each one of us in different directions. By all means, it is during our growing days that the magic happens—when the inspired mind awakens the inner-power to lead the way and invites hope, courage, and aspiration to fulfil its purpose.

Prologue

In the eyes of a child, the world is a playground; all that matters is making friends and what game to play.

~ The Author

The earlier part of my life as with every child was wonder years in many ways. My cousin Egbichi was my best friend and the sandy playground was ours to enjoy—whatever game we chose to play. In the light of day, we felt safe and secure because we'd been told in the church that Jesus was our friend. But in every dark corner and in the darkness of night, we felt surrounded by ghosts, and every bit of noise scared us to death, so we clung to each other for protection.

My village celebrated different events such as the new yam festival and Christmas with dancing masquerades. Few carried flames on their heads; some had the profile and carved ornaments of an angel. Dibias walked around with strange-looking accessories and oxtails everybody believed to have magical powers. To innocent children, both the Dibias and the masquerades possessed magical powers they could use to destroy anything in their path, so we watched from a distance.

Growing up, we did not have electricity in the village, and nobody cared because it was just something they had in the townships. But we had our own special light—moonlight in which we'd play until we got exhausted then we'd run down to the water and bath before going to bed. Making friends and playing different games was all that mattered. During Christmas celebrations, people who lived in the township came home with lanterns to light up their homes. Then we'd gather to admire the festive light.

I suspect that some readers may find this book nostalgic. I plead "No contest." How could it not be? It is often tempting to view a person through the narrow lenses of his success without considering how he began his life, the pathways, and obstacles he overcame before realizing his success. Some children start life with a clear path to success and others with no chance at life because their parents cannot afford their education.

The later was my plight growing up. So when I think of the present, consider the past, and look back at the road that led to this moment, I can't help but marvel at how gracious and merciful God is.

My inspiration to become electrical engineer came when two American scientists, Mr. David Marshal, and his companion Mr. Henry Anderson conducted a demonstration on the production of electric light in my school classroom and invited me to turn on the light. Yes, I was blown away by the flood of light that illuminated the dark class.

It turns out that inspiration alone is not sufficient; it has to be accompanied by hope, courage, and aspiration to become real. I had graduated from primary school and left home to live with my brother in the township of Aba to learn how to trade—buy and sell jewelry.

Without any doubt, my life was heading in that direction with nothing to aspire to except, maybe, to get rich, which I cannot claim to have entered my mind. Then my standard six (sixth grade) teacher, the principal of Alayi Methodist Central school invited me to return home; next, my uncle Emeke Chima asked me to an interview for the job of an elementary school teacher—within one week.

When I went home and met Mr. Madubike Okocha, he had filled out an application for me to take the entrance examination to the *Government Trade Center*, Enugu. He paid my travel expenses to attend the two rounds of the entrance examinations and even shuttled me back and forth between his house and the train station in the town of Ovim. In the end, I passed the entrance examination, and I was admitted to the school. I also attended the job interview and got the job. I can honestly say that it was my uncle's persuasion and my teacher's love and kindness that encouraged me to aspire to that one thing—to become an electrical engineer. Hence the title of this book: *The Courage to Aspire*. I have added a glossary of Igbo words; used in this book to help readers understand the meaning of those African words.

Chapter 1
Peer Applause

You learned right away that applause sounds like love.

~ Ava Dellaira

Amigwu is a small village in the town of Alayi located in the southeastern region of Nigeria now known as Abia state. The main occupation was farming, so everybody farmed in one way or the other—mainly for subsistence. Alayi seemed quiet. Serene, undisturbed, and at a distance from the hustle and bustle of the city—a place where people respected the elderly and went about their business. Villages were organized in compounds; row houses of various shapes and ample sandy space which allowed children to play in front of their homes when the playground—the square is occupied.

Each compound was named after its founder—man or woman. The name of my village; Ufundierimma means the home of the descendants of the founding mother—mama Erimma. That's where I was born, and I was proud of it.

My dad was very proud of mama Erimma even though he never knew her. For lack of interest, I never bothered to ask Dad why he idolized the woman he never met. I can visualize the look on his face if I had asked. The playground in my compound was sandy and soft, so my cousin Egbichi and I loved to play there more often than at the square even when other kids were playing there.

Egbichi and I had been born on the same day and at the same time of the day—a few minutes apart. Our parents were best friends; we had learned to crawl and walk together.

"You and Egbichi spoke your first words just about the same time," my mom had told us.

"I don't believe it," I had argued.

"It's true—both of you said 'Maa' at the same time. Ask Mama

Chuks I. Ndukwe

Anya," she said.

Egbichi and I loved to play in that rich sandy playground, and we took turns playing different roles. One Sunday afternoon, when we were three going to four, she lay on the sand and spread her legs.

"Draw me," she said.

I traced her body. And then I lay next to her figure and spread my legs.

"Draw me too," I said.

We inspected both figures to see if there was any difference between them. We drew eyes and mouth on both characters. Then We looked at the characters again, laughed and fell over each other. When we stopped playing, Mom came out and screamed at us,"You're not coming in my house covered with sand like you've got no sense."

We dusted the sand off each other.

"Let's go to the stream so you can take a bath," Mom said.

We were riding on each other's back when Uncles Okereke Chima, Azik Ukachukwu, and a huge tall man walked into Dad's house.

As I was dusting off the sand, Dad called out, "Ogbuleke, come in here."

I told Egbichi to go home because I did not want her to cry if she saw me being spanked. I knew I'd be punished if Dad didn't like the way we were playing.

"Come over when you finish," she said.

I went inside the house looking dusty with sand all over my body. The huge tall man stood up.

"What is your name?" he asked.

"Ogbuleke," I answered.

"My name is Mr. Okpee," he said.

My uncle stood up and took my right hand and put it over my head. He asked me to touch my left ear. I tried, and I wasn't close.

The huge man and my uncle tried to make my right hand reach my left ear; they bent my head until I began to feel pain in my neck. Suddenly, they said together, "Yes, he touched it."

"Why do you want this child to touch his ear? You almost broke his neck," Dad said.

"The Methodist church wants to start a new school at the church,

The Courage To Aspire

and we don't have enough children to make up the required number," my uncle said, "so we would like Ogbuleke to attend the school to help us make up the required number." "We know that a child is ready for school if he or she can touch the left ear with the right hand," the huge tall man said...

"He's not ready for school yet," my dad said, as he brought out a jar of palm wine, which he had tapped himself. Mom served them yams and vegetables. When they finished eating, I ran to Egbichi's house. I was excited by the prospect of going to school.

"Uncle Okereke wants me to start school in his church," I said.

"Do you want to go?" she asked.

"Yes, Mom said it was OK," I replied.

Egbichi grabbed her mom, sobbing.

"Maa, Ogbuleke is starting school. I want to go with him," she said.

"Is your uncle still in your dad's house?" Mama Anya asked.

"Yes, he is still there," I answered.

Mama Anya went to Dad's house and came back with a smile on her face. "Both of you will be going to school together."

Egbichi and I hugged each other, screaming and jumping up and down until we fell on the ground. Then we got up and went back inside the house. We ran around and told our friends, even the ones we did not like to play with.

Mom's stomach had gotten big; she kept telling me there was a baby in her stomach. A few days later, I woke up in the morning, and women were singing and dancing in my compound. "Your mom had a baby this morning. Go and see the baby in the bedroom—his name is Anyele," Dad said. At first, I was bewildered; I wondered how that baby came out of her stomach. But when I saw her carrying the baby smiling, I was happy, and my stunned mind calmed down. I sat next to her, shaking the baby's tiny, soft hand. Women came in groups and congratulated Mom. Mama Anya stayed over for four days and cooked for us.

Egbichi's dad had died when she was one year old, so Dad was her surrogate dad. Before the school opened, Dad bought slates, chalk, and had our uniforms sewn by the tailor. Mine was a white shirt, and brown shorts and Egbichi's was a white blouse and brown skirt. We were ready for school and talked about nothing else but starting school.

Every Sunday we wanted to know when school would start.

"Mama Nwaka, is tomorrow a school day?" Egbichi asked often.

"No, it's not tomorrow," she said.

The thought of going to school made us feel grown, so we began to learn how to feed my baby brother and to hold him on our laps. Carrying the baby was as much fun as playing in the sand as long as he did not poop or burp. When the baby did, I simply vanished, but Egbichi had no problem helping Mom clean the baby up.

One Sunday after Christmas, Egbichi and I were playing at the square and enjoying roasted beans and coconut. Suddenly, Egbichi pinched me. "Those people are going to Papa Ikebie's house," she said.

Uncle Okereke, Azik, and Mr. Okpee strolled across the square to Dad's house.

"Let's go home," I said.

When we got home, we sat by my dad's side, hoping to hear that school would open the next day. Dad brought out undiluted palm wine, and Egbichi and I gave out cups. When they finished drinking the wine, we helped Mom prepare the Sunday meal. Mom was in an unusually cheerful mood, my baby brother was sleeping in the bed, and we were anxious to hear from the visitors.

We were helping her clean up after the meal when she broke the news and said, "You are starting school tomorrow."

Egbichi and I dropped what we were doing and ran straight to Mama Anya and told her.

I stayed awake all night, anxious to put on my school uniform. "I am a big boy now," I said to myself.

On Monday, I woke up early before everybody, including Mom.

"Maa, wake up," I said and shook her.

"Ogbu, what are you doing waking up so early? Go back to sleep," she yelled.

"I want to go to the stream and take my bath; it's time to go to school," I replied.

"No, it's too early. I will wake you up in the morning," Mom said.

I went back to bed, grudgingly. I simply stared at the underside of the thatched roof, waiting for Mom to call my name. Suddenly, Mom

The Courage To Aspire

tapped me on the shoulder. "Ogbu, wake up," she said.

I jumped up, ready to walk to the stream, but she had my baby brother in her arms, which meant she was not going anywhere.

"Go and wake Egbichi up. I have a bucket of warm water for you two to take your bath," she said.

When I got to her house, she was sleeping, and her mom was cooking.

"Mom wants both of us to take a bath at my house," I told her mom.

"OK, come back and eat before you go to school," she said.

We ran to my house. Mom was preparing food for us too.

"Mama Anya wants us to eat at her house," I told Mom.

"OK, I will wrap this up for you to take to school for lunch," she said.

We went back to Mama Anya's house and ate the breakfast she had prepared specially to make us happy. It was our favorite breakfast: *akara* (fried balls of dough of black-eyed peas) and *akamu* (creamy blend of corn flour). We put our uniforms on, feeling proud and excited. Mom escorted us to the village square. We stood there, wondering why she wouldn't let us go. We waited and waited until we got restless.

"Stop jumping around," Mom said.

"Why are we standing here?" I asked.

"We are waiting for Jeni."

Suddenly, a tall woman approached us. "Mama Nwaka," she called out.

"How are you?" Mom greeted.

"Mr. Okpee instructed me to pick these two kids up. I will walk with them to school and back every day," she told Mom.

"Yes, I know; that's why we are waiting for you. I will have food waiting for you on your way back from school; come to the house," Mom said.

We walked to school with the tall woman behind us; sometimes, she held our hands. When we got to the church house, there were kids all over the green grass. It was intimidating to play with those kids, who were much older and stronger than us.

"Put your bags down and join your mates," the tall woman told us.

Chuks I. Ndukwe

We played for a while, and then Mr. Okpee blew his whistle and asked us to form two lines. We marched back and forth while he yelled, "Left, right, left, right." Finally, he directed us into the church house.

"My name is Mr. Nnaji Okpee—you can call me Mr. Okpee—and this is Miss Jeni Okorie. You can call her Miss Okorie," Mr. Okpee told us.

Miss Okorie spent some time teaching us a song for our morning assembly, and Mr. Okpee said the prayer. We got divided into two classes. I was in Mr. Okpee's class, and Egbichi was in Miss Okorie's class. We were disappointed about not being in the same class.

Miss Okorie marched her class to the far end of the church, while Mr. Okpee's class took the front end of the church. It wasn't so bad. Egbichi and I could see each other from our respective seats. On the first day, we sat on the floor, and the teachers sat on their chairs. I sat in the front row and was happy to have a front seat so I could see Egbichi in her class.

"This is your permanent seat," Mr. Okpee announced.

"This is how we will sit every day," Miss Okorie announced to her kids.

We took turns telling our favorite folk stories. Some stories were very familiar, and others were totally new. As the kids came up to tell their stories, I began to like a few of them just from the kind of stories they shared and how they told the story. Some kids really made the class laugh.

Suddenly, Mr. Okpee called my name. "Ikebie, it is your turn," he said.

I told a story about O'motar and the tail people; it was a famous story, so most of the kids knew the story. When I got to the part that involved singing, the whole class joined me in singing the song; I could see Egbichi looking in my direction.

I wished she were in my class because she liked the story too.

When the bell went off again, we took a short break. During the break, kids gathered around me and told me that they liked my story. When we returned to the class, the two joined together.

"You must bring a stool, slate, and chalk to school every day," Mr. Okpee said.

The Courage To Aspire

We sang the song Miss Okorie taught us, and finally, the school was over. When we got home, Mom was cooking yams and vegetable sauce.

"How did they do?" Mom inquired.

"They did well," Miss Okorie replied.

"Did they fall asleep?" Mom asked.

"No, they had lots of energy."

Mom served us the food. "Get water for your teacher," she said.

"I'd like to get it; she's my teacher," Egbichi said

"OK, you can get it," Mom replied.

After eating, Miss Okorie held my baby brother for a while, and then we escorted her down to Igwu with Egbichi and me holding hands and hopping along on both sides of the road. When Dad came home, I told him that Egbichi and I needed stools to sit in the class.

"That's what Mr. Okpee said."

He walked into one of the rooms and came out with two little chairs. "Here are the stools," he said.

I went to Egbichi's and gave her one of the chairs.

"Keep it in your house. I don't want Mom to break it," she replied.

"Why did you say that? I asked. "She doesn't need a small chair like that."

"She sits on mine when she is cooking and breaks it all the time," she said.

"You are right; she sits on one when she is making *akara*," I said, thinking about the golden, fried dough of black-eyed peas she served for breakfast.

The next morning we waited for Miss Okorie to meet us at the square.

"Here she comes," Mom said.

We looked around, and she was walking up the hill. Before we left for school, Miss Okorie held my brother for a few minutes.

"You must be ready for hygiene first thing every morning," Mr. Okpee announced. Dirty kids were given a note for their parents and sent home.

On Tuesday, Miss Okorie came on time, so when we got to school, we had ample time to play with other kids. Now that we were getting used to the other students, Egbichi and I began to make friends. Instead of playing with me, she ran straight to a group of girls who were holding hands and moving in a circle. I joined some boys who were kicking a soccer ball around.

One day in December, Mr. Okpee announced that there would be a final examination. He posted the date on the wall.

From that today on, there was no storytelling or dancing. We practiced and practiced everything we had learned in the school year. On Friday, Mr. Okpee informed us that the examination would start on Monday.

On the last day of school, we gathered in the church. After the opening prayer, Mr. Okpee called the names of the kids who were being promoted to elementary two.

"Those who did not hear their names will repeat elementary one," he said.

Egbichi's name and mine were not called, so we thought we had failed the examination. Then Mr. Okpee continued. "The first in my class is Ogbuleke Ikebie, and the first in Miss Okorie's class is Egbichi Ejere." He picked us up and let us stand on top of his table.

"Clap for them," he said.

The school clapped, and we were dismissed for the Christmas holidays. Only three kids had failed the examination.

On our way home, Miss Okorie held our hands while we bounced up and down. We got back home earlier than usual, and Mom hadn't cooked yet. Dad was home too. It was *Eke*—native's market day and nobody goes to the farm on that market day. Miss Okorie stopped briefly, played with my brother, told Mom and Dad how I did in the final examination and left.

On Sunday, Dad sold out his diluted palm wine in the morning, but he saved one jar. So I knew he was expecting some visitors in the afternoon. Soon after Dad finished with his wine sales, I saw Mom plucking *oha* leaves—just enough to cook with. When she finished with that, she began to grind *ukpo'h* nuts. Then she brought out a big dried fish and put it in the water. It was evident that influential people were coming to visit.

"Maa, who is coming to visit?" I asked.

The Courage To Aspire

"How did you know?" she asked.

"I saw Dad save his special jar of undiluted wine," I answered.

"Uncle Okereke, Azik, Uncle Jeremiah, and headmaster Okpee are visiting after church service," she explained.

I stayed home to help her watch my brother. Later on, Egbichi came over. When she finished cooking she said to us:

"Come on, you two, let's go to the stream so you can take your bath and look decent when your headmaster comes to visit."

"Mama, who is that?" Egbichi asked.

"Mr. Okpee," I answered.

"Oh," she mumbled.

When we came back from the stream, churchgoers were just coming back from church.

"Go and put some clothes on before the visitors come," Mom said.

I put on a polo shirt and black shorts, and Egbichi wore a white blouse and a black skirt. We looked like we were going to church. We did not wait for long before Uncle Okereke, Uncle Jeremiah, Azik, and Mr. Okpee arrived.

"Ogbu, come and greet your headmaster," Dad said.

Egbichi and I walked gingerly to Dad's house, not knowing what to say. As we walked inside the house, Uncle Okereke beckoned us to come to him, and he embraced us.

"I heard how you two did in your examination—well done," he said.

"They are going to elementary two when school resumes," Mr. Okpee said.

"Didn't you say that they were too young to be registered?" Dad asked.

"Well, the headquarters in Ovim did not oppose their promotion," Mr. Okpee said.

We shook everybody's hand and ran out quickly. Dad called us back to pass *nzu* (a slab of chalk) around, according to the custom. Dad told me once that the offer of *nzu* signifies peace—a welcoming symbol. It is the first thing a visitor is offered. After *nzu*, we passed out cups that Dad filled with palm wine. At the end of the evening, we escorted our visitors to the village square and shook their hands.

Chuks I. Ndukwe

✳✳✳

One day before the beginning of the new school year, Mom's friend Ogbonne came over and told Mom that Egbichi had left early that morning to live with her brother Mba leaving me to wonder about how I could go to school without her. However, Mom did not waste any time; she pulled out her tender-loving-care magic and calmed my bewildered mind down.

When we started class the next day, Miss Okorie inspected our hands, ears, hair, teeth, and clothes. One girl, Ejije Aka, was dirty, so she was sent home with a note for her parents.

"We have gone through the vowels enough. Now we are going to start on other alphabet letters," Miss Okorie announced. We did, and classes continued. On Easter Sunday, Miss Okorie came over and took me to church. After church, all the teachers went to Uncle Okereke's house. I stayed with his wife, Mama Ugo, while the teachers and Uncle Okereke ate and drank wine. They chatted and laughed loudly, and I wondered why they were so happy. Later Dad came and joined them. He was still there when Miss Okorie and I left.

One afternoon on our way home from school, Miss Okorie and I stopped at my village square to play soccer. It was awkward because boys did not like to be seen playing soccer with a woman. Nevertheless, I went ahead and played with her. Surprisingly she knew how to play soccer. SO we chased and dribbled the ball around each other till I got tired.

"I am tired; let's go home," I pleaded.

"Just one more time," she replied.

Finally, she picked up her books, and we went home sweating.

"Why are you two sweating?" Mom asked.

"We've been playing soccer at the square," Miss Okorie replied.

We sat down and cooled off before Mom served food. After eating, Mom and Miss Okorie chatted for a while, and then she left. On the last day of school, we scrubbed the classroom and the blackboards and piled our chairs on top of the desks. When Mr. Okpee rang the closing bell, we marched into the church, then Mr. Oji, Mr. Ume, and Miss Okorie led us in singing as loudly as we could, clapping, and dancing. After the

The Courage To Aspire

opening prayer, Mr. Okpee called out the names of kids in elementary two who'd be transferring to Methodist Central School to start standard one; I was one of them. Then he called out the names of kids in elementary one who would be promoted to elementary two. "If you did not hear your name, you failed the examination, and you will repeat your class next year. Merry Christmas; you're dismissed," he said.

Chapter 2
First Step Forward

Not all those who wander are lost.

~ J. R. R. Tolkien

School had just ended, and I had reasons to be happy and look forward to attending Methodist Central School, but I wasn't. Something was bothering me. From my village, I could see the central-school location on top of a very high hill. The thought of climbing it every day was on my mind, and I was scared.

I woke up one morning as the hazy sun hung in the sky, unable to warm the village. Fog hovered everywhere in the village. My skin looked dry and ashy, and I was afflicted with a scratchy cold. It was just about that time of the year when elders set up burn fires (big piles of wood scraps that the villagers kept burning from dawn to dusk) at the village square. They sat around the fire and roasted yellow yams, which they ate with hot palm oil. Dad had been talking about it too. When I looked up, the sky was filled with *aku* (an edible insect) flying around and falling down in bunches.

Mom called out to me. "Ogbu, go out and pick some *aku*."

I ran out to the square; there were people everywhere struggling to knock the insects down or catch those flying low enough to be detected. I joined the crowd, and I picked some from the ground. The brownish flying insects—the size of locust—were difficult to catch. I looked around and realized that everybody had a basket or bag in which to put the insects, so I ran back to my house and asked Mom for a container to put the insects in.

I returned to the square and spent a good portion of the morning, chasing after insects. I filled my bowl, which was some kind of condensed-milk can. When I got home, I gave the container to Mom.

The Courage To Aspire

"You did well. Sit down," Mom said. "I will fry them for you."

I sat down in the kitchen, and I waited for her to fry the insects impatiently. When she finished and gave them to me—they tasted like nothing I'd ever felt before. Then I went back to the square to catch some more. By then, the game was over; aku had stopped falling. Every morning when I woke up, I waited for *aku* to fall, but they did not, even when the weather seemed to be ideal for them to fall. For weeks I waited in vain. The sun still hung in the sky, and the fog got denser, and the only thing left to do was to sit around the fire and enjoy the chilly morning.

One Sunday morning Miss Okorie came by while I was sleeping, and the thought of going to church was the last thing on my mind that morning. Nevertheless, Mom came to my room and woke me up.

"Ogbu, Miss Okorie is here," she said.

I thought she was joking. I was still on my Christmas holidays, and the school hadn't opened yet, so I had no teacher at the moment. I curled up and around and covered my head with my mat. Then she removed my cover and left the room. But still, I wrapped myself again.

"Get up. Jeni is here to go to church with you," she repeated.

I jumped up. Miss Okorie was sitting on the opposite side of the room, holding my brother.

"Ikebie, get up; it is time to go to church," she said.

"Good morning, miss," I greeted her.

I took a quick bath and left for church with Miss Okorie. At church she read the Bible that morning, and my uncle delivered the sermon. When we came home, Miss Okorie spent some time with us talking about the new school year and how she couldn't wait to see the kids running around the church and in the field.

"The Methodist Central School has a better and larger field than Amankalu Methodist School. You will enjoy it," she said.

"I will escort him to school on the first day of school," Mom said.

"Splendid idea," she replied before leaving.

On the day school began, Mom got me ready wearing my old uniform. When Dad came home from wine tapping, I left for school with Mom. We climbed that dreaded mountain of a hill from Igwu all the way to Amokwelu. It was a long walk, and the road was decorated by nature with beautiful flowers on both sides. I was surprised Mom did not hold my hand while we climbed the hill. However, I was tempted to grab her hand, but the beauty of the flowers distracted me, also many kids were walking with us, and nobody was holding their hands. When we got to the top of the hill, I turned around and looked down the slope; it was so deep and steep that I couldn't believe I'd climbed all the way to the top.

"It will be easier on your way home," Mom said.

"Why?" I asked.

"You will not waste as much energy as you did climbing the hill," she said.

When we arrived at the Methodist Central School, Mom asked somebody to show her the headmaster's office; the man looked like one of the teachers too.

"Where should I take my child for registration?" Mom asked.

"Where is he transferring from?" the man asked.

"From Amankalu Methodist School," she answered.

"Wait till the school starts; the headmaster will announce it," he said.

We sat down on the long wooden bench under the tree. After the assembly, the headmaster came to the bench where we were sitting.

"Are you here for registration?" he asked.

"Yes, I want to register my son. He attended Amankalu Methodist School for two years," Mom said. "He passed his examination, and Mr. Okpee told us that he'd be attending school here this year."

"He has been registered already," the headmaster said.

He showed us the standard-one classroom. Mom and I walked inside the classroom, and a few kids were sitting in the class, waiting for the teacher. Those kids were the ones who had failed last year's final examination. The new students gathered outside the classroom. The teacher arrived with the register in his hand. He called the names of each kid and showed him or her where to sit. Mom waited until my name was called, and then she waved and went home.

"My name is Mr. Igbokwe, I am your teacher, and this is class one A," he announced. "Where you are sitting now will be your permanent seat for the entire year. Your uniform will be a white shirt and khaki

The Courage To Aspire

shorts, you will bring your slate to school every day, and I will supply you with chalk."

Unlike in the elementary school, green grass covered the large campus. Boys and girls shared everything except sports and restrooms. There were fewer girls in my class because villagers valued boy's education more than girl's. We could only walk along the walkways that connected the teacher's quarters and two gates to the six buildings—each containing two classrooms; four of the buildings formed a quadrangle. There were lots of rules to obey, and any violation was punished by spanking with a thin, long stick. When Mr. Igbokwe finished explaining the rules, he called every kids' name.

"I want you to come to the front of the class and tell us your name and which village you are from," he said.

Kids walked up to the front of class one at a time and introduced themselves to the class. When it came to my turn, I went in front of the class.

"My name is Ogbuleke Ikebie. I am from Ochufu," I said.

"No, you are from Amigwu," Eme, my friend interrupted—embarrassing me.

"Amigwu is the name in the register—not Ochufu."

Shortly, the bell rang for lunch.

We played until the bell went off again, and then we lined up and marched to our respective classes. As Mr. Igbokwe was calling the roll, the big man who had shown Mom and me, my classroom came into our class.

"Class, salute," Mr. Igbokwe ordered us.

"Good afternoon, sir." We saluted.

"Be seated," he said.

He walked back and forth, and then he finally stood still and looked around.

"My name is Mr. Okocha, and I am from Umuahia. I am the headmaster of this school, and I also teach standard six. My house is the first house on the right from—the road," he said. "School will be closing now, so you can go home and get the appropriate school supplies and the right uniform. Starting from Monday, I will send you home if you do not wear the right uniform."

School closed without assembly, and kids ran out of the classroom as if they had been held captive.

It was awful; Mom had not told me what to do when the school closed or how to get home. I stood in front of my class, thinking about what to do next, then I walked outside. I had a few options. I could walk to Mr. Igbokwe's house and ask him how I could get home, or I could simply follow a large group of kids walking in one direction. What if the group I chose were going the wrong direction home?

I was about to cry, but then an older boy from my village, Ugoji Kanu called out my name.

"Ogbuleke, school is closed. Let's go home!" he yelled.

I ran back to the classroom and picked up my lunch box, and then I joined his group. We walked around the quadrangle along the walkways then we headed toward the gate. Kids were chatting as we walked along, especially the girls; they talked about their new teacher, the kids spoke of teachers they did not like, and the ones they had hoped to be assigned to. I was not interested in any of that, so I walked along quietly. When we got home, Mom was standing in front of our compound, waiting for me.

"Thank you, son, for looking out for Ogbuleke," Mom said to Ugoji. "I forgot to tell him how to get home after school. Thank you."

"Ogbuleke, when you get ready in the morning, wait for me. We will be going to school together every day," Ugoji said, and then he continued to walk up the hill to his house.

Mom patted me on the head gently.

"How do you feel? Was it easier coming home?" she asked.

"I don't know; kids were chatting and pushing one another. I didn't know when we reached our village," I answered.

We walked inside the house, and she had food ready for me, but it wasn't like when I was coming home with Miss Okorie. I ate by myself and went to sleep. The first day of school at Methodist Central School was not that horrendous after all. When I woke up, I told Mom that I needed a new uniform.

"When do you need it?" she asked.

"Monday," I replied.

"OK, I will give you a signal after dinner to tell your dad."

The Courage To Aspire

"Maa, what is the signal?"

"When I look at you and nod two times like this," she said.

After dinner, Mom looked at me and nodded twice.

"Our teacher said we have to wear new uniforms on Monday; anybody who does not wear the new uniform will be sent home," I said to Dad.

"OK, after school tomorrow, your mom will take you to the tailor at Amoji Square to have your measurements taken," he said.

When we got home the next day, I gave my schoolbag to Mom and continued on to the tailor's shed at Amoji with Ugoji. This was the only place we could get our uniforms and formal clothes made because we did not have malls or stores that sell ready-made garments. When we got there, nobody else was at the tailor's shed, so he took our measurements immediately.

"Your uniforms will be ready on Saturday," the tailor said.

When I got home, Mom had my food ready for me. Therefore, I ate and went to sleep.

Waking up, Anyele was sitting on me, slapping me with both hands as if he was trying to wake me up. I felt his soft baby hand and grabbed him and played with him for a while before going out to the square to play with my mates.

From that day onward, we strolled back and forth to school in groups as the big boys protected the smaller kids from being picked on.

On *Eke*—the market day that villagers rested from farming every eight days—elders sat around the square and watched market goers as they streamed past the village in one direction in the morning and in the opposite direction in the evening. I was sitting at the square with Dad when Mom and Mama Anya left for the market.

"Don't forget to pick up Ogbuleke's uniform," Dad told Mom.

Everybody was out watching kids play soccer when Mom returned from the market. Getting home after the game, Mom was giving my brother a bath in the backyard. "Your uniform is on your bed; try it on, and show it to your dad," she said.

I put it on and showed it to Dad; he nodded in approval. Then I ran to the backyard and showed it to her too.

"You look handsome," she said.

Chuks I. Ndukwe

The following afternoon, when I went out to play at the square, I did not feel excited, so I watched other kids play.

Getting home, I stopped at the sandy playground. And It was no longer the happy place it used to be before Egbichi went away to live with her brother.

"Ogbu, your brother is calling you," Mom said.

I turned around, and my brother was babbling and waving at me. I ran to him as Mom was standing him up. I held his hand and helped him take a few steps. I looked at Mom, and she seemed happy, as she always did whenever I played with him. I helped him walk to the sand, and we played until he was covered with sand.

"Don't let sand get in his eyes!" Dad yelled.

Before I could say anything, he had started to eat the sand.

"Maa, come here! Anyele is eating the sand," I said.

At that time, Anyele was starting to get teeth, so it was not safe to stick anything in his mouth to get the sand out. Mom pressed his jaws together with two fingers and unstuffed the sand from his mouth. Thank God Mom was around; I would not have been able to do that. She took Anyele to the backyard and gave him a bath.

On Monday I had my old uniform on, and Ugoji had his new outfit on.

"You are wearing the wrong uniform," he said.

"The headmaster said that we must wear the right uniform on Monday," I said.

"Today is Monday," he said.

So I changed my uniform, and then we walked together to school. Going to school had become a routine, and the mighty Amokwe Mountain was not so terrifying anymore.

When classes started that morning, Mr. Igbokwe passed out chalk, and we began regular periods. The bell rang at the end of every period in succession until the lunch break.

After the break, we lined up again and marched into our classes. We'd started to learn the alphabet, and Mr. Igbokwe liked to teach it with songs. It did not take long before I got hooked on the "ABCD" song. I sang it until I could sing it in my dreams.

Mr. Igbokwe's brother, Christian—or Chris, as he liked to be

The Courage To Aspire

called—was in my class and we had become friends. So when it was time for manual labor, Mr. Igbokwe told him to go home with me and clean his house. Sometimes Mr. Igbokwe came home when the school was still doing manual work and prepared food for us. We ate and waited for the closing assembly bell to ring, and then we came back to the class and joined other kids. Going home from school was always riddled with surprises. Boys in my group loved to tease and mess with girls from other groups, and boys in those groups returned the favor by teasing and messing with girls in my group. Every tease was met with defensive measures.

For small kids like me, it was kind of fun to see the big boys going at it; we cheered and jumped around. It was immediately obvious whom the small kids were cheering for; just the moving of hands and yelling and standing in each other's way made it look like sport.

At school, Chris and I had become close friends. We played and went everywhere together. Sometimes we sat under the mango tree and talked. He loved to talk about his village in the town of Isu. He never got tired of talking about his dad and his mom. I also spoke of my village, Amigwu, Mom, and Dad too.

On Monday morning, we had a joint assembly in the juniors' soccer field. And there Mr. Okocha made the following announcement; "There's going to be a soccer match on Friday between Methodist Central School [my school, which was located in the area of town dominated by the Methodist Church] and Roman Catholic School [which was located in another section of town dominated by the Roman Catholic Church]. I expect the school and our classrooms to look spotless."

After that announcement, the atmosphere became effervescent, and kids went into a state of frenzy. The anticipation alone was enough to drive anybody who was not a student of the Methodist Central School crazy.

When I went home, I told Mom about the match.

"What time is the match?" she asked.

"I don't know. I think it will be in the evening; that's when the team play soccer." I didn't know exactly when the school played matches. I had never watched one before.

"Why can't they play it during the school hours?" she asked angrily.

"Maa, everybody will be there. I want to go too," I said in a subdued voice.

"I don't think your dad will be happy to hear that you will climb that monstrous hill twice in one day," she said.

"Tell him that everybody is going," I said.

"Your dad doesn't think about everybody; he thinks about what is right," she replied.

"Maa, I can stay with Christian until the match starts, and after the match, I will come home with Ugoji and other kids," I said.

Dinnertime did not come fast enough. Dad was home, and he seemed to be in a good mood. He played with my brother, throwing him up and catching him on his way down; the boy giggled and looked like he enjoyed it. After dinner, Mom told Dad about the match.

"All the kids are going. Ogbuleke can stay with his friend till the match—that way he doesn't have to climb the hill twice," she said.

"That's OK with me," Dad answered.

I couldn't believe how easy it was for Mom to convince Dad to allow me to attend the match.

On Friday, after the morning prayer, the headmaster announced, "The school will close at noon, so the players can have time to prepare for the match."

Mr. Igbokwe was one of the players himself. When Mr. Igbokwe walked into the class, he did not salute the class as usual. Instead, he sat for a while, and then he went over to Mr. Mbakwe's class, and both of them walked out together to the game master's house. We were on our own, throwing chalk at each other, and suddenly the end-of-school bell went off.

It did not take long for the school to empty out as students headed home through various gates in larger groups than usual. I followed Christian home; we ate lunch and played soccer in his backyard and then took a nap. When we woke up, students in black-and-white uniforms were walking around the school and inside the classrooms.

"Look, those are the Roman Catholic School students," Christian said.

The Courage To Aspire

"Where are they coming from?" I asked.

"The other side of the road," he answered.

Finally, our players—in black-and-white jerseys and followed by our headmaster—walked to the field. Christian and I trailed at a short distance. When we got to the playground, the two teams were kicking balls around at the opposite ends of the field. After a while, the referee entered the field and blew the whistle. Two players approached the referee, he conducted the coin toss, and the game was on. I walked around looking for Ugoji.

As I was walking past our goal area, somebody blindfolded me. I knew Christian would not play such a trick on me, so I kept quiet and waited for the trickster to say something. He didn't for a minute, and then the crowd broke out in a loud roar.

"We've just scored," Ugoji said.

We jumped up and down. I was happy to have found Ogoji, and we watched the game together. At halftime, Ugoji bought groundnuts, and he gave me a handful. We ate and walked around the courthouse until the game started for the second half.

A few minutes before the end of the match, our team scored the second goal, sending our students into absolute pandemonium while the visitors stood frozen like giant pieces of rock. When the referee blew the final whistle, the visitors walked out of the field slowly while our students stormed the field, cheering and jumping. I had never been that happy. We walked home in one large crowd, singing and clapping. When we got to my village, I ran to Mom, screaming, "We won, we won!"

"Sit down and eat your dinner. You must be hungry," Mom said.

After dinner, I tried to tell Mom how good our team was, but she wasn't interested, and that made me sad.

"Why can't she be happy for me? This is the first big thing that has happened in my new school; she should at least be happy for me," I thought.

Two weeks later, the final examination started, with teachers from different schools conducting the final exam, which lasted for a week, and after the exam, teachers spent two more weeks grading the tests. During that period, we ran wild in the bush, picking some fruits known as abaa—which was black on the outside with a kernel that turned yellow when it was ripe for eating. We walked to the motor park, Ozara Desert, Ezialayi Valley, and beyond. Seniors who were graduating from standard six came to school looking casual.

On the final day of the school, we had a joint assembly. The headmaster announced the names of students who were graduating and those who were being promoted to higher classes. I was one of those who passed. At the end of the assembly, the school closed. Kids who had failed the examination cried all the way home, while those who had passed tried to comfort them.

Chapter 3
Leaving Home

It is always sad when someone leaves home unless they are simply going around the corner and will return in a few minutes with ice-cream sandwiches.

~ Lemony Snicke

My first year at the Methodist Central School was much better than expected. I wasn't sure that I'd fit in with the kind of students I saw every morning boisterously streaming past my village, often nudging each other. Being so small, I was afraid they would crush me on the way to or from school, but nothing like that happened. Instead, I fitted in nicely with that wild crowd, and surprisingly, made friends.

I was glad I passed the final examination and excited I'll be in a higher class next year, but disappointed teachers did not announce the names of kids who scored first, second, and third. It would have been nice to know. On Sunday, Miss Okorie came by, and we went to church together.

"Ikebie, how did you do in your final examinations?" she asked.

"I don't know, but I'll be promoted to standard two next year."

"I wouldn't be surprised if you came first or second," she said.

Mom prepared breakfast; we ate and left for church. Predictably, she held my hand as usual. I wanted to pull away from her but did not for fear she might be offended. After church, we chatted with Uncle Okereke for a while; he was glad to hear the result of the final examination. When we returned home, Mom had prepared the Sunday meal and was waiting for us. Later, we escorted Miss Okorie to Igwu.

"Jeni really likes you," Mom said.

I did not say anything. By that time, hearing that was boring and Mom's baby-like treatment, hand-holding, and patting-on-the-head annoying.

Chuks I. Ndukwe

At the square, kids talked about those who had failed the final examination and about kids who were going abroad, to spend the Christmas holidays with their relatives. Ugoji was one of the kids; he was going to Aba for the holidays.

On Monday, Ugoji stopped by on his way to the motor park to board a lorry for Aba, to spend the holidays with his uncle. I escorted him to Igwu all by myself for the first time. We waved at each other, and then he climbed Amokwelu hill until he was out of sight. Then I returned home.

Another good friend who did not travel abroad, Kanu came by, but playing with him was not always fun. We loved to argue, and sometimes we fought over minor issues—such as who would take which part of the square when we played soccer and whether a tackle was foul or not. One evening, we fought until we got tired and lay side by side to cool off.

"Do you still want to play?" Kanu asked.

"No, I don't want to play anymore," I replied.

I cannot remember when we walked together like friends. Our idea of bathing was throwing water in each other's face and wrestling in the water. We were age mates, but we were not born on the same day. I was born a few days after him, so he claimed to be older than me because he was born first. Therefore, he tried to order me around, but I never let him have his way. For that reason alone, we fought always.

One day Dad talked about it. "You should never let that boy push you around; his father tried the same thing with me. The only way to settle that kind of conflict is at the wrestling ground."

I did not know what he meant by conflict and did not ask for his explanation. I never felt comfortable asking him questions like I asked Mom. In the evening, Mom served dinner. While we were eating, Dad asked Mom.

"Do you remember when Okoro and I used to wrestle until elders separated us during wrestling competition?" "We struggled for domination over one another, and neither of us was willing to cede an inch. That's what is happening between your son and that boy, Kanu Okoro."

"You are right; I've seen both of them fighting like dogs," she

The Courage To Aspire

replied.

Despite constant pushing and fighting, Kanu and I grew closer, to the point that we stood up for each other when anybody tried to pick on either of us. I did not forget what Dad said about settling a score on the wrestling ground, though. I watched older boys when they wrestled, and learned some techniques and postures that successful wrestlers used to throw their opponents down. I was preparing for the day when Kanu and I would face each other on the wrestling ground.

One evening, Kanu came over as I was drawing a dog on the sand. He came from behind and grabbed me without saying a word. I twisted my waist and threw him down. He got up and dusted the sand off.

"Are you trying to prove that you can wrestle?" Kanu asked.

"Why did you scare me like a cat?"

"OK, let's wrestle."

"I don't want to wrestle."

"Are you afraid I'll humiliate you in front of your father?"

"No, I don't feel like going to the stream to take a bath."

"You don't want me to beat you; admit it," he said.

I got up and looked at Dad; he winked and nodded. Then I dusted the sand off my body.

"Did you say that you want to wrestle?" I asked.

"Yes."

"OK, I am ready; let's wrestle."

We locked heads, and he tried to grab my waist. I pushed him off, then he tried to get hold of my neck. I slipped away. I had seen his moves with other kids, so I knew what he was trying to do. I pushed him back.

"You have one more chance," I said.

He got mad and came at me with a vengeance.

He grabbed my neck with both hands, and then he got down on his knees and pulled me down, so both of us were on our knees with nobody gaining an advantage. We struggled and struggled until we got up again. I pushed him back.

"OK, you've had your chance; now it's mine," I said, breathing heavily.

"What are you going to do?" he asked.

Chuks I. Ndukwe

I had watched Uncle Ogba Ochu wrestle Kanu Nwefere several times, so I decided to throw Uncle Ogba's technique at him. I bent down, leaning forward as if I were picking something off the floor. I moved toward him, then back; forward and back again, and then I charged at him with force, grabbing his legs and throwing him down. He got up quickly.

"Again, I wasn't ready," he growled.

"I am done wrestling," I replied.

"I want to wrestle again," he insisted.

"No, I gave you a chance. It's not my fault that you got beaten."

"OK, when you come over to my house, I'll crush you," he said.

"You did well; he's not going to threaten you anymore," Dad said in a tone that suggested approval.

The realization that I had just humiliated Kanu set in. However, despite his threat, I wasn't scared. Still, going over to his house to apologize seemed a friendly thing to do.

"Don't be silly. That's how it's supposed to be; from now on, Kanu will give you the respect you deserve," Dad said.

Mom set up a bucket of water at the backyard for me to take a bath. After helping Mom to serve dinner, she leaned closer:

"I didn't know that you could wrestle like your father," she said.

"He did well. I am proud of him," Dad added.

Mom went on and on about how people Dad's age were afraid to wrestle him when he was a young man and had two good legs. (Dad lost his left leg when he jumped in a burning fire to rescue his friend).

"Your father won lots of wrestling competitions," she said.

I could not believe Mom and Dad were happy about the humiliation Kanu went through. The following day everybody was home. It was *Eke* market day, and girls were everywhere on the square selling things like *akara*, *maimai*, roasted groundnut, and stylistically peeled oranges. Mom sent me to buy *akara* from Sister Ugo. Getting there, Kanu was standing by his sister, eating salted peanut she had roasted in an ashy fireplace.

"Ogbuleke, taste this groundnut; my sister roasted it," Kanu said.

"This is pretty tasty," said I.

Kanu did not seem angry anymore. Nevertheless, I bought a few

The Courage To Aspire

rolls of *akara* and went home. Mom did not go to the market that day. She did not have *gari* or palm kernel to sell, so we sat around the house and luxuriated all morning.

✳✳✳

One Saturday afternoon, two weeks before the beginning of school, I ran into Ugoji's mother on her way to the stream.

"Ogbuleke, Ugoji is coming home today. I will be going to the motor park to wait for him in the evening," she said

"Can I come with you?"

"Ask your mother," she replied.

I ran home as fast as I could, excited about the prospect of standing around at the motor park to watch Ugoji get off the lorry and embrace his mother and me.

"Maa, Ugoji is coming home today. Can I go to the motor park with his mother to wait for his arrival?"

"Your father will not like that," she said.

I sat at the square dejected and waited until I saw two people walking up the hill hand in hand. There was no doubt that the image was that of Ugoji and his mother, so I ran down the slope, staggering a few times, before getting close to them.

"Hello, Ugoji!" I screamed.

He ran forward and lifted me up.

"Ogbuleke, you should have been there. Aba is a wonderful township; we played both in the day and at night in different soccer fields. We walked around at night and visited confectionery stands where women and girls sold everything under electric light." He could not stop talking.

We walked to his house hand in hand. He gave me a loaf of bread and distributed pieces of bread to other kids who came to welcome him back. Before leaving his house, he gave me a slingshot, which is what we called catapult. He knew I wanted a catapult to shoot down mangoes like other kids did when we found red ones. I went home and showed Mom the gift and shared the bread with Anyele.

Chuks I. Ndukwe

When I woke up the following morning, the only thing on my mind was shooting down either birds or mangoes with the catapult. I went out to look for the birds that perched on the branches of orange trees by my house, chirped, and flapped their wings every day. I did not see any of them. They were not on the trees and not in the backyard. Frustrated for not finding any bird to shoot at, I aimed at some banana trees and shot stones at them. It was thrilling to be able to shoot at anything. I hung the weapon on my neck for everybody to see. Obviously, it was an excellent position—like all the kids who carried catapults everywhere they went, always ready to shoot down any game that came their way.

The last week of the holidays brought excitement and anticipation. Some kids got new uniforms, while others kept their old outfit. The next morning, Ugoji came by the house, then we walked to school in the usual large group. Some teachers had not come back yet, so we did nothing but play all week long. On the following Monday morning, we arrived at school very early and began to clean the teachers' quarters. While we were cleaning Miss Azubike's building, I went inside her kitchen to remove the ash in the cooking place, and her sister, Erika, was collecting firewood to cook breakfast.

"Do you do this every day?" she asked.

"No, only when we arrive at school early," I said and left quickly after cleaning the kitchen before Miss Azubike woke up.

After the morning assembly, we marched to our respective classrooms and settled in our seats, then Miss Azubike walked in with a small staff and introduced herself.

"My name is Neka Azubike," she said. "I will be your teacher for this school year, and I will call the roll first thing every morning, so try to be in class before the roll call, OK?"

Walking home was quite orderly; there was no quarreling. I wondered if the school year would be different from the previous—when two or three kids fought or pushed and shoved each other every day—on the way home.

When I got home, I could not play with Anyele because he had a fever. It was awkward eating without him dipping his fingers in my food. I did not go outside to play either. I was concerned that he would get worse if I went out to play.

The Courage To Aspire

"Go and play with your friends," Mom encouraged.

"No, I don't want to play."

"Go and play; he will be OK," she insisted.

At the square, everybody was talking about their teachers. Older kids knew the good and the not-so-good teachers, but Miss Azubike was a new teacher, so nobody knew anything about her.

At dinnertime, Dad asked about school. "How was school today?"

"It was good," I answered.

"Pay attention to your teacher," he advised.

On Easter Sunday, Miss Okorie came by, and we took off for church. When we arrived at the church, we took our seat on the pew beside two elderly couple.

"Look who's coming to church," she said.

I turned around. Miss Azubike, Mr. Mbakwe, and another woman were just entering the church. They walked in and sat beside us. Miss Azubike sat next to me. I sat still—shy of sitting between two of them and unable to move or say anything. I stood up when they did and relaxed when they sat. I looked straight without turning my head. Mr. Okpee attended, but he did not take an active part as he usually did. He just sat there as our presiding elder.

Typically, Miss Okorie would give me money to put in the offering-tray, but on that day, I was not sure she would give me any money. As the offering-tray moved toward us, I felt like walking out of the church, but without a word, Miss Okorie put money in my right hand, and Miss Azubike put cash in the other. It was awkward; I did not know how to say thank you to both of them at the same time. Finally, the tray reached us, then I dumped the money in the tray with both hands.

When church ended, a few people hung around to speak with the preacher, and teachers lingered around to chat. They stopped by Mr. Okpee's house before we left the church. On our way home, Miss Azubike introduced me to her mother.

"Maa, this is one of my pupils. His name is Ogbuleke Ikebie," she said.

"What a nice little boy," she said.

"Maa, this is Miss Okorie. She was Ogbuleke's first teacher," Miss

Azubike said. Then they exchanged pleasantries.

Mrs. Azubike held my hand as we walked home, while Miss Azubike and Miss Okorie chatted and Mr. Mbakwe did not say much. When we got to my village, Miss Okorie invited everybody to meet Mom and Dad.

"These are Ogbuleke's parents and his baby brother, Anyele, and these are Ogbuleke's teacher at the central school and her mother, Mrs. Ada Azubike," Miss Okorie said.

"Please sit down," Dad said.

Dad had undiluted palm wine, and Mom had prepared her Sunday meal. I ran after Mom into the kitchen, scarcely believing what was happening. She smiled at me; I knew she was happy but did not know why.

"Go and set out the plates," she said.

I set the plates and water out for them, and then I ran back to the kitchen.

"Sit down with us," Miss Azubike said.

"I am not hungry," I replied.

"He'll eat in the kitchen," Mom intervened.

After the meal, we escorted the visitors to Igwu and came back home.

When we returned to school after the Easter holidays, I went to clean Miss Azubike's kitchen. As I was removing ash from the cooking place, Erika walked in.

"My mother left today. She said that she met your parents, and wants you to visit her during the midyear break," she said.

When classes began, Miss Azubike told the class that she had attended Amankalu Methodist Church on Sunday.

"I met Ogbuleke in the church, and after church, we ate with his parents," she added. "His father makes the best palm wine."

On Fridays, when the whole school did manual labor, Miss Azubike invited me to go with Erika and fetch water from Amokwe Spring—drinking water that runs out of rocky-hill-side.

In June, after the midyear examination, Miss Azubike wrote a letter to Mom and Dad telling them she wanted me to go home with her for the holidays.

The Courage To Aspire

Mom and Dad approved, and Mom got my clothes washed, laid it out to dry in the fresh air, and packed a small bag for me. On the last Friday before the break, Mom gave Ugoji the bag to carry. When we got to school, I went straight to Miss Azubike's house and gave Erika the bag.

"Don't go back to the class; stay here and help me pack. We will be going home in a car shortly," she said.

"Let me tell Ugoji."

I ran to the classroom and told Ugoji I was going away with Miss Azubike and went back to help Erika pack. Then we ate fried plantain and beans and waited for Miss Azubike to come home. When the school closed, Miss Azubike came home in a white car. We put our luggage in the trunk and left for midyear break. We drove straight to her home in Isukwuato, and her mother picked me up like I was a small baby. I spent the week with her family: playing soccer with kids in her family and helping Erika and her mother with everything possible.

Throughout the break, Miss Azubike was very much out of sight. As for Erika, she was out with her friends most of the time, but whenever she was home, she took me around the village to see her friends and relatives. I kept company with Mrs. Azubike when she sat in the living room knitting—and helped her with garden work too.

At the end of the break, as we were getting into the car, Mrs. Azubike hugged me. "You are a delightful boy," she said. We returned home late on Sunday, so I slept over at the teachers' quarters with Erika. Early in the morning on Monday, Erika and I swept around the building and prepared breakfast for Miss Azubike; then we went to school.

When classes began, Miss Azubike announced the names of kids who had failed the midyear examination and encouraged them to work harder. On the way home from school, I was filled with joy and anxious to see Mom. It was my first time leaving home. When I got back home, Mom hugged me, and I grabbed Anyele and tickled him as he tried to run away. At dinner, when I told Mom and Dad about the trip, Mom simply did her head-rubbing-routine and smiled without saying a word.

In late November, we took our final examination then teachers spent two weeks marking and grading the scores. On the last day of school, the prefect rang the closing bell, and students converged on the junior soccer field. After the closing prayer, each teacher read the list of students in his or her class who failed the final exam. Those who passed did not all hear their names, but the first ten names were announced in their order of merit and were loudly applauded. In my class, Eke Okai took the first place, Elechi Uche came second, and I came third.

"You did well. My mother will be happy to hear that," Miss Azubike said.

Chapter 4
A Lesson in Reality

If there's a single lesson that life teaches us, it's that wishing doesn't make it so.

~ Lev Grossman

✳ ✳ ✳

I had hoped to be first in every examination. For that reason, anything short of first place was a failure. The stubbornness of my belief disavowed any hostile coexistence between expectation and reality. As in every child's mind, expectation trumps everything. I wanted to be first in the class and expected to be. I was the smallest and the youngest student in the class, but in my mind, nobody was bigger or older than me.

When the result of the final examination was announced last year, I felt as though I was a failure. I was not happy to hear I was third in the class. Lost in the how-to-and-when to break the sad news to Mom and Dad, tears flowed, and disappointment took over as I wondered what their reaction would be. On the way home from school that morning, kids who had failed the examination cried, and those who had passed expressed some kind of jubilation, hopping from one side of the road to another.

Getting home, Mom was not back, Dad had left for work, and I was at home all by myself. I lay down and covered my head with my lunch bag. I tried to go to sleep, but the thought of ranking third in the class would not let it happen. Suddenly, I heard footsteps.

"Look, your brother is home already," Mom said to Anyele as they entered the house. I just lay there and did not say anything.

"What's wrong? Are you OK?" she asked.

I got up slowly and took my brother from her. I threw a fake punch at him and tickled him as he tried to run away as usual. I pursued him until he ran into Mom's arms.

"You came home rather too early today," Mom said. "Oh, I forgot; it's the last day of school. How did you do on the exam?"

"I wasn't first in my class, and I am not happy about it."
"OK, did you pass?"
"Yes, I came third," I replied.
She put Anyele down and picked me up like a baby. "You did very well," she shouted.
"Maa, I am not a baby. Let me go; other kids will see us."
As soon as she let go, I ran away from her, but it was too early, so nobody was at the square to play any kind of game. I went back home reluctantly, hoping she was done with excitement—especially the picking-up, at eight years old. Dad came home from the farm—planting fruits and vegetables; he went right back out with a pot in his hand, without sitting down even for a second. I knew he was going to the swampy waterside to start a new wine tapping, so I followed him.
"Where are you going?" he asked.
"I want to go with you."
"Water is a little too deep where I am going—few more years," he said.
In the kitchen, Mom was cleaning a big fowl.
"Maa, what are you doing?"
"I am getting ready to cook chicken soup with *oha* and *ukpo'h*."
"Who is coming to visit?"
"Nobody—just for us," she said.
I salivated and wondered if Dad would be kind enough to give me the head and legs of that fowl to share with Anyele; by tradition, children ate legs and the brain.
When Dad came home, food was ready for dinner. He did not know what Mom cooked, but the sweet aroma from the kitchen filled the air and gave away Mom's secret. Usually, Dad ate whatever Mom cooked without asking questions. But this time, he looked at me as if to say, what is going on? I knew he expected me to disclose the secret, but I did not say a word.
"Nna Dick, are you ready for dinner?" Mom asked.
Mom never addressed Dad by his name; instead, she called him as a father of his first son, so "Nna Dick" means father of his son Dick. (Dick was my older brother. He lived abroad with Uncle Emeke, and we had not met yet).

The Courage To Aspire

"Yes, I've been ready since I walked in and smelled something," Dad said.

"Ogbu set out the plates," she said.

I set the plates out for everybody, and Mom served soup and *foo-foo* in their respective plates and the big fowl on a separate, large plate with a sharp knife lying next to it.

"Nwakaku, what is the occasion?" he asked. That is how he addressed Mom when he was happy and romantic.

"End of the school year—your son came third in his class," she explained.

"Is that true?" he asked.

"Your nephew, Okereke Chima, will be thrilled to hear that," Mom said.

"Don't worry; I will have the best wine saved for him when he comes over on Sunday," Dad said.

Mom knew how to transform a sad situation into a celebration.

On Saturday, Dad made sure Uncle Okereke got the news. After church service on Sunday, Uncle Okereke, Azik, Okorie, and Mr. Okpee came over as we were playing in the square. I ran and grabbed Uncle Okereke's hand, and we walked home together as always. He did not ask any questions; instead, he talked about the church service.

"Your headmaster preached the Gospel today," he said.

When we got to my house, Dad gave me *nzu* and cola nut to pass around; then I passed out cups for palm wine. They joked and laughed while they drank.

"Does anybody have a question for the young student?" Dad asked humorously.

"Yesterday was the last day of school. Could the young scholar tell us how he did in his final examination?" Mr. Okpee asked. Hated that question and almost sprinted outside.

"Not well, sir. I came third in my class," I said.

"How many students did you have in the class?" he asked.

"There are Thirty-six students, sir."

"Brilliant," he said.

"Why do you think you did not do well?" Uncle Okereke asked.

"I wanted to be first."

Chuks I. Ndukwe

"Next time," Mr. Okpee said.

After the meal, I escorted the visitors to Amoji village square and chatted with Uncle Okereke for a few minutes, and then he did the pat-on-the-head like Mom.

"I will send for you next Sunday to come and spend Christmas with us," he said.

"Are you happy now?" Mom asked when I got home.

"Yes, Maa, I am."

On Sunday Mama Ugo came by, and we left together.

I spent a week with them, mostly helping Mama Ugo in the kitchen. After a week, I returned home with a few gifts, including a school uniform and some dried nuts. It was nice to be home because when I was away, there was nobody to play with. Uncle Okereke lived in a big house close to the church but away from the village, so there were no kids around to play with.

When I returned and visited Kanu, he was not happy that I had left without telling him.

"Mama Ugo came by and took me home immediately," said I.

"Let's go to Umuosiala," he said.

"Why?"

"I'd like us to visit Ugoji."

When we got there, Ugoji told us his sister had graduated from teacher-training college.

"She will be one of the teachers when school opens," Ugoji said.

When I heard that, my anxiety level rose.

"She is going to be your teacher next year," Kanu said, laughing.

"Is that why you wanted us to visit Ugoji?" I asked.

"I thought you should know," he said.

On Monday, Miss Kanu and Oyidiya joined us as we walked to school together. When we got to school, we cleaned the teachers' quarters before joining other students to do the morning cleaning. After classes had begun, Mr. Eleke ran into the classroom.

"I'm sorry I'm late; our car didn't leave Igbere in time," he apologized.

He called the roll, and we began the period. Our subjects that day were reading, arithmetic, writing, and English. No subject gave me as

The Courage To Aspire

much difficulty as writing; I could not get "j" and "y" to curve correctly at the bottom or "f" to curve correctly at the top. I spent lots of time with Oyidiya at home, learning how to write.

The most comfortable subject for me was arithmetic, and to my surprise, most of the students found arithmetic very difficult but wrote perfectly well. On Wednesdays, we had combined a singing lesson with the standard three B class. The singing lesson was more fun than most other subjects. I did not know why; maybe it was because it led directly to the closing assembly, and when we left school, we sang the song all the way home.

One Monday in May, Mr. Eleke began to review previous lessons when nobody was talking about the midyear examination yet. He gave us tests every day. During that period, we focused on preparing for the midyear examination. I studied during lunch breaks and immediately after school because we did not have good light for studying at night.

One early morning in June, we had a combined assembly on the junior soccer field. After the opening prayer, the headmaster announced, "Midyear examination will start on Monday of next week. You have a whole week to prepare. Good luck."

On Friday, we arranged the classrooms for the midyear exam as a part of our manual labor. Oyidiya invited me home, and instead of going to the stream, we studied for the midyear exam.

"Are you ready?" she asked.

"I am not sure."

"Why?"

"I did not do well last time."

"You came third in your class."

"I was supposed to be first."

"Why are you obsessed with first place?"

"That's what I want."

"Just passing the exam should make any normal person happy," she said.

I hated preparing for exams because of the anxiety and stress it brings with it. I studied writing all through the weekend. I feared that one subject the most.

On Monday, we went to school with nothing; teachers supplied paper and pencil at the beginning of every test. The examination started with reading for standard three. The teacher wrote ten words on the blackboard and called each student into the class to spell and pronounce those words. Then the student went out through the back exit and stayed at a designated place to prevent those waiting outside from finding out what went on inside the exam room.

The examination ended on Friday with writing, and school closed for midyear break two weeks later. I went home, determined not to worry or talk to anybody about the examination. On the way home, some senior students bragged.

"The exam was easy. I finished in half the time allotted," some seniors said.

"I know I scored one hundred percent in mathematics," others said.

I was amazed that some students could be so sure of how well they did in any examination while freaking out was all I did.

On Saturday, it rained all day nonstop. It rained almost every day from June to September—rainy reason. We played in the rain diving in the flood of the rain pretending to be swimming.

Playing in the rain was the kid's favorite thing, so we could not get enough of it. After dinner, I went to bed hearing "pit, pat, pit, pat" on the roof all through the night. It helped take my mind off the worries of the midyear examination.

On Friday, each teacher read the names of students in his or her class who had flunked the examination. When all the teachers had finished reading the names, the headmaster praised us for helping the class prefects to maintain order when the teachers were marking the examination papers.

"If you did not hear your name, you passed the midyear examination," he said. "If your name is one of those called out, you have to study hard. Enjoy your break; you are dismissed."

It was only a midyear examination, so there was not much cheering or crying; we simply went home happy to be staying away from school for two weeks. On Saturday, Oyidiya and Miss Kanu came home. Oyidiya was furious that we did not check on her and Miss Kanu before going back home on Friday. She loved to play in the water, so we lured her to the stream. As soon as she finished changing her clothes, we

The Courage To Aspire

threw her in the water and then we jumped on her.

"Do you forgive us?" Ikpo asked.

"Yes, I forgive you," she said.

Finally, we dried ourselves and went home for dinner.

One day in July, we had just taken our seats after the lunch break when the classrooms began to shake, and the gray clouds became very dark. The wind blew dirt, books left on top of the desks, and easels in the classroom around. It was chaotic; a torrential rain had begun to fall, as the wind grew stronger and blew water into the classrooms—because the walls were only four feet high. We all got wet. Mr. Okocha walked around in the rain without an umbrella—from one class to another, guiding students—with the aid of their teachers—to the senior classroom, which was the only building with walls reaching the roof. As soon as the rain stopped falling and the high wind subsided, school dismissed. Then we went home all drenched.

When we got home, parents were anxiously waiting to see their children. They had experienced the same rare occurrence.

"Are you OK?" Mom asked. "Oh, you are soaked wet. Let me take your clothes off." Probably every mother was saying the same thing. She took my clothes off, prepared pepper soup, I ate, and then went to sleep. When Dad came home, he was also soaked, so everybody had experienced the same stormy weather.

Nothing happened in the town without a superstitiously charged rationale. In this case, villagers scrambled to come up with the reason for the storm.

Shortly, the elders concluded that *Chukwuobioma* was sending a message of some sort. The only problem was that they failed to identify what the message was and to whom it was directed. The English interpretation of *Chukwuobioma* is "God of mercy." *Dibias*—followers of *Chukwuobioma* went to work.

"One of the reasons for the torrential rainfall and high wind was bad behavior of the high priest. He has offended *Chukwuobioma*," some concluded.

"Young people were deviating from the traditional culture," others said.

In the end, they agreed that the resolution was for the *dibias* to perform a ritual in which they killed a goat or fowl and smeared the blood on their *agwu*—a shrine for offering sacrifice to *Chukwuobioma*.

So they chose *Eke* for the ritual, every *dibia* killed a goat and sprayed the blood on their *agwu* with a libation to *Chukwuobioma*.

It was a great day, as Dad sold out his wine quickly, and kids ate lots of goat meat.

In August, not too long after the message from *Chukwuobioma*, the village celebrated the new yam festival, and every *dibia* killed a goat or fowl and offered the blood to their *Ofo'h*, "the protector of homes." *Dibias* came out in full force to display their magical proficiency. Two *dibias* would face each other, and with a wave of the hand, handkerchief, or cow tail, they sent the opponent staggering—and in some cases falling down.

I wasn't quite sure why such displays were necessary, but the popular belief was that they wanted to prove they still had their magical and healing powers.

On Friday, seniors repaired parts of the broken school fence ripped apart by the high wind, girls fixed the flower beds, and the juniors scrubbed classrooms and repainted the walls.

November was always a magical time of the school year. Rain rarely falls, and the sun hangs high in the sky while fog covers the whole town, making everything look mysterious. Schools challenged each other to soccer matches.

One day in November, during morning assembly, the game master announced; "We invited Amokwe Item Methodist School to a soccer match, and they accepted," he said, "so we will be playing against them on Friday next week. I ask every student to attend the match and support our team."

Our team practiced every other day, harder than they ever did before; probably they wanted to revenge the last year loss. Last year Amokwe Item beat us by three goals to nil. On the match day, school dismissed at noon to give every student enough time to come back for the match. I stayed with Oyidiya. Ugoji had joined the school team, and he and his team-mates slept in the standard-six classroom. Then they went to Mr. Ebeneza's house to eat and bathe.

Suddenly, Amokwe Item students began to arrive traversing the full

The Courage To Aspire

length and breadth of our school. We could see them roaming from classroom to classroom as if to see what we were up to. The visiting team gathered at the courthouse, and we could see them from the teachers' quarters.

Eventually, the headmaster came out with Mrs. Okocha, and Mr. Ebeneza came out with our soccer players. Miss Kanu, Oyidiya, and I joined them and went to the soccer field. There was a little apprehension on our part. First, the opposing players looked stronger and bigger than our players and second they had beaten our team last year. We hoped this match would be a payback. The headmaster seemed to have a spring in his steps, which was maybe a sign of confidence.

When we got to the field, our players dashed onto the playground and occupied one end of the field. Then the visitors ran out of the courthouse and took another end of the field. They kicked the ball around for a while, then the referee blew the whistle, and the captains joined the referee at the center for a coin toss. After the second whistle, the two teams took their positions, and the match started. A few seconds into the game, the visitors took complete charge of the game, passing and dribbling the ball from side to side, forward and back. Our team sat back as if to figure out the opponents' strategy. The other team's movements were swift and precise. Suddenly, they broke through our defense and struck the ball; luckily, they narrowly missed our goal.

Our goalkeeper took the goal kick, sending the ball into the visitors' eighteen. Elowo trapped the ball, and then he turned around and with his left leg, he fired the shot through the opponents' goalposts. The atmosphere became electrified, cheers broke out, and we could even see the headmaster jumping up and down. Energized by the score, our players took control. They kept the ball without moving in a clear direction, thereby frustrating the visitors' defense. As the first half was winding down, our players drove the ball backwards toward our goalposts, and the opponents dashed forward for an attack. Mr. Eleke sent a long shot ahead to the right end, and Eze received the ball and went into the attack. He tried to dribble past the opponents' defense, but they stopped him and kicked the ball out of their end.

The referee awarded our team a corner kick. Then Mr. Ebeneza

Chuks I. Ndukwe

took the corner kick, landing the ball right into the opponent's goal area. After a short scramble, Ugoji tipped the ball past the opponents' goalkeeper, sending our students into pandemonium. At the half, the score stood at Alayi Methodist Central School two and Amokwe Item Methodist School nil. When the match resumed, our players changed their strategy and mounted an impenetrable defense.

At the end of the match, the score remained Alayi Methodist Central School two and Amokwe Item Methodist School nil. It was an act of sweet revenge. I wanted to sleepover at Miss Kanu's house, but Ugoji wanted us to go home, so we went back with other students, singing and cheering.

Two weeks later, the final examination started. Teachers from nearby schools came and took charge of the tests, and some of our teachers went to other schools to conduct theirs too. On the last Friday of school, the assembly bell went off as early as nine o'clock. When Mr. Eleke announced the results for my class, I was the first in the class and so happy and almost ran out of the assembly area.

After the assembly, I went to Miss Kanu's residence, and Ugoji was already there. He was also happy that he and Oyidiya were among the first ten in their classes. We went home together with Miss Kanu feeling happy.

After dropping off my lunch bag, I continued with my best friend, Ejere Igwe to his home. He was from Amachi, and they have the cleanest stream. Some days, we went fishing together after school and came home with drinking water. Mom and Dad liked him, so we hung out a lot.

Chapter 5
Fear Of failure

Our greatest fear should not be of failure but of succeeding at things in life that don't really matter.

~ Francis Chan

On every last day of each school year, my head was overloaded with anguish, agony, and a crushing headache. I discovered that the suspense, uncertainty, and inevitable result of the final examination—compounded by the venue and method by which teachers announced it—could force a child to suspend play and enjoyment of life and to yield to the fear and agony of failure.

I learned that expectation and reality often diverge even when their convergence is all but assured. Going home on that day presented its own unique challenges. The overly excited and happy kids who were rewarded for their exceptional performance found themselves in an awkward situation. The balancing act of encouraging the less jubilant kids and consoling the sobbing kids made going home together on that day the most dreadful of all things a child can go through.

Last year I had not been happy about coming third in the class; this year, I took the first place I had always wanted; still, I could not express my joy. I was unable to reconcile painful and conflicting emotions. So I ran into the bush, pretending to be depositing body waste until the crowd was far ahead. Then I came out and strolled behind them. When I got home, Mom was not there; she had gone to the waterside to fetch drinking water that flowed out of a rocky hill.

She came home carrying a pot of water on her head and a basket of mpataka—thin slices of fresh cassava—in one hand. I loved mpataka with coconut. So when I saw her, I rushed forward and took the basket from her.

"Where is Anyele?" I asked.

"He is with Mama Anya," she replied.

Chuks I. Ndukwe

When we got home, she put the pot and the basket away; then we went to Mama Anya's house and came right back with Anyele. She cracked the coconut and gave us some with mpataka. Anyele liked mpataka too. I did not go out to play that day. Instead, I stayed home and played with Anyele.

On Saturday, Oyidiya came by. She stayed for a while and played with Anyele, pinching and tickling him like I used to do.

"Ogbuleke, I am going to school to bring Miss Kanu's belongings home. Would you like to go with me?" she asked.

"Let's ask Mom," said I.

"You can go," Mom replied.

In the afternoon, we went to school and brought Miss Kanu's belongings home.

On Sunday Azik, Uncle Okereke, and Mr. Okpee visited after church. Dad had reserved a specially diluted palm wine for the occasion. I was the bartender, and they drank and chatted while I refilled their glasses. I loved to bartend so I could hear what they talked about—and they talked a lot.

That afternoon they talked about the examination and about the day, they had twisted my right hand to get me to touch my left ear over my head.

The next morning, I could not get out of bed. I felt weak and tired.

"Are you ready for breakfast?" Mom asked.

"Yes," I answered.

A little while later, breakfast was ready. The golden rolls of akara were still in the frying pot, and Mom was stirring the milky-looking akamu. I set the plates quickly.

"Here, it's for you and your brother," she said, filling the plate with the akamu.

"I don't want to eat with Anyele? He is too greedy," I snapped.

"OK, let me put his in a separate plate; keep eyes on him," Mom said.

In a minute, Anyele's mouth was full of akara, and akamu was dripping on his body and on the floor—off his spoon.

"Maa, come here fast," I called out.

"What do you want?" she asked.

The Courage To Aspire

"Come look at Anyele."

Without waiting, I dragged him over to her and went back to my seat.

"I don't want to eat with him anymore; he doesn't know how to act," I repeated.

I went back to enjoying my food alone while he went to the backyard to clean himself up.

In the evening, Dad came home late, so we waited for him until bedtime. He walked in singing and staggering.

"I stopped by my nephew's house to discuss some issues, and he wants Ogbuleke to come over and spend two weeks with them," he said unapologetically.

On Sunday, I went to church with Uncle Okereke and Mama Ugo and sat with the choir. That was the most fun part of my time with them. To me, singing in the choir meant you are a true worshiper of God. I was a child, and every child's decision should not be subject to questioning, so I decided to join the choir as soon as I was big enough to do so. On Christmas Day, I went to church with Miss Kanu and Oyidiya. Ugoji did not come with us; he'd gotten hurt playing soccer. Christmas carols made me happy and joyful, so after church, I kept singing all the way home. Mom had invited Miss Kanu to Christmas dinner. So when we got back, Mom had a bowl of rice, and fowl stew waiting for us.

"Come and sit down. I have been waiting for you," Mom said.

We sat down and enjoyed the traditional Christmas meal: rice and fowl stew. Then after lunch, I followed Miss Kanu and Oyidiya home and ate again in their house. That was the tradition on Christmas Day: you ate rice wherever you went.

That year the farming area was very close to the village. It was so close you could see people working in the farms, and vice versa. Men had just begun to clear the bushes. They either carried food with them, or they came home for break. Every afternoon, Mom went to the farm with Anyele and me to eat lunch with Dad. Some days we stayed with him until closing time; then we took a bath in the stream and came home together. It was fun; Anyele and I ran around in the bush chasing each other, and most kids were doing the same.

Chuks I. Ndukwe

Mom and Dad had a family tradition: on Wednesdays, they worked on Mom's vegetable patches. There was no way to know which plot belonged to one or the other; the only way to tell was which plot they worked on Wednesdays.

On Wednesday, we woke up very early, brushed our teeth, and went to the farm. Dad cleared some space in the bush and built a small tent for Anyele and me, and Mom built a fireplace for cooking. I picked Anyele up and said to him;

"OK, big boy, they are serious; we are going to live here forever."

While I was preparing a space in the tent for Anyele to sleep, Mom had already gone to Ogba to fetch drinking water.

"Here, this pot is drinking water, and that pot is for cooking and washing our hands," she explained.

She joined Dad, who had already cleared a large portion of the plot. I watched both of them hitting the plants and the tree branches with a vengeance.

"Maa, I want to help," making my way to where she was.

"Watch your brother," she yelled.

I did not understand why she was yelling; I was only trying to help. They had cleared half of the plot when people began to pass by.

That was the first time the whole family went to work together. Mom was in a good mood—judging from the way she was cutting everything down with her sharp knife.

"Ogbuleke, get me water," Dad said.

"No, I will get it," Mom said.

She rushed to the tent, filled the cup with water, and gave it to Dad.

"Maa, I am hungry," I yelled out.

She looked at me, abandoned what she was doing immediately, and prepared food for us. Farmers ate when they felt hungry. Mom roasted yellow yams and served them with hot palm oil. After the meal, they rested for a while before they resumed work.

Dad returned to work first, then Mom followed. They attacked the bush, cutting plants and trees down until the sun took a dive into the west, and plants began to cast their shadows all over the farm. We packed up and took our bath before other farmers arrived to join us at the stream. When we got home, I was exhausted even though I did not

The Courage To Aspire

do any work at the farm. I managed to stay awake for dinner, and then I went to bed. I woke up the next morning, to itchy hands and legs, and furious scratching.

"Why are you scratching?" Mom asked as she inspected my body.
"I don't know why I am itching," I replied.
She looked at my hands and my back.
"Give me your hands; mosquitoes bit you yesterday," she said.
She rubbed oil all over me, including areas that were not itching. When Anyele woke up, she examined him and did not find a single mosquito bite.

"Thank God I did not see any mosquito bites on your brother," she said.
"Nna Dick, what do you want for breakfast?" she asked.
"Nothing, I am about to leave the house right now," Dad said.
"You work too hard; you must eat before you leave the house," she said.

She peeled yams, ground pepper, and prepared pepper soup. Dad ate before he went to work. It was surprising how Mom overruled Dad's decision every single time. She did not have a loud and robust voice like Dad, but her sweet, mild voice had a much farther-reaching impact than his. I did not ask her how she manages to control Dad like that, knowing that she would smile and perform her head-rubbing routine. That was her way of saying, "Son, you are too young to know." When Dad left for work, I escorted him to the edge of the square and came back. Then we swept the compound together, and then I played with Anyele until we fell asleep. When I woke up, the village was as quiet as a ghost town; all the kids had gone to the farm with their parents, as I did the previous day.

On Monday, the first day of school, we defied the cold weather and took a bath in the stream. When we got to school, I was assigned to Standard Four A, and the new teacher was Mr. Nwabeze. I had hoped to be in his class for long, so my wish came true. Mr. Nwabeze was handsome, light-skinned, and tall; everybody liked him for his friendly smile.

When he got to the classroom, he was smiling.
"My name is Amechi Nwabeze, and I will be your teacher for this

school year," he said. "Your task is to pay attention to me while you are in this classroom and to listen to everything I say, and my job is to teach you and help you to understand what I am teaching. Is that clear?"

We sat down quietly while he compiled the list of all the books and materials we needed for the year. When he finished, he went around the classroom and handed the list to each student.

"I'd like to know each one of you, so come up and introduce yourself and tell us what part of Alayi you come from," he said.

I started, as I did in every class.

"My name is Ogbuleke Ikebie, and I am from Amaigwu Amankalu Alayi."

"Clap for him," he said.

The introductions went on until we got to the last student in the class. Elendu Iheke was still standing in front of the class, introducing himself, when the bell rang for a lunch break. A few kids ran out, but Mr. Nwabeze called them back.

"Nobody leaves the classroom while I am sitting here unless I say so; is that clear?" he asked in a harsh tone that made him seem mean.

During lunch, a few kids expressed surprise about his meanness before the break; it was good to know that other kids felt the same way I did. After lunch, he called the roll, and every now and then, he bent over and looked at a student from the top of his eyeglasses. It was hard to tell whether he did that to see the student more clearly or to frighten him or her.

For whatever reason, the image of him looking like that stuck in my mind. After the roll call, he stood up.

"I want to go over a few rules you may not be accustomed to," he said. "I run a tight ship, so I like to impart discipline to my crew, I will not keep you in the classroom any longer than it is necessary, so when the bell goes off for leaving the classroom for any reason, you must remain seated until I ask you to leave. Did I make myself clear?"

"Yes, sir," we answered.

"For the rest of the afternoon, I want you to come up and tell the class all about the last Christmas holidays. Don't be shy. When you finish, I will tell you all about mine. Let's start with Ikebie," Mr. Nwabeze said.

The Courage To Aspire

"During the holidays, aku fell; we ate lots of it. On Christmas Day, I went to church with Miss Kanu and Oyidiya and Ugoji; then we ate rice. I spent two weeks with my uncle Okereke Chima, and sang in the choir with Mama Ugo," I said.

"Clap for him," he said

"Did you do anything else?" he asked.

"Yes, I went to the farm with Mom and Dad and Anyele too."

"Next," he said.

Each student then told the class how he or she had enjoyed the holidays. When the last student finished with his story, the closing bell rang, but Mr. Nwabeze had yet to tell his story. Therefore, we sat and waited for him to tell his story.

"Well done, everybody. Time has run out; we will continue tomorrow," he said.

The following day, Mr. Nwabeze came into the class beaming.

"Yes, I promised to tell my story about the last Christmas, so here I go," he said. "A day after school closed, I traveled to Enugu, the capital of the Eastern Region to spend the holidays with my brother. Enugu is a beautiful city with the house of assembly sitting on top of the hill and the secretariat scattered around it. I went to work with my brother every day and strolled around the capital. Vendors set up tables all over the place to sell everything. I visited the governor's mansion and worshipped at the Anglican Cathedral on Christmas Day. Finally, I watched the soccer match between the Nigerian Eagles and the Gold Coast All-Stars. It was magical; the game ended with a one-to-one draw. Finally, when I returned home to Ovim, I went to the farm a few times with my mother before coming back."

We clapped and clapped for him. We were proud that our teacher's brother worked at the Eastern Regional capital. He must be one of those people they called "honorable," we concluded.

After Mr. Nwabeze's story, the bell rang for physical education.

"Let's go to the junior field and stretch ourselves," he said.

We marched to the junior field and competed in different kinds of races. For size or strength, I was no match for the other kids; I always lost by a few yards. When the bell went off, I went to lunch with my friend, Innocent.

Chuks I. Ndukwe

"Let's go to the courtyard," Innocent said.
"Why?" I asked.
"My mother sells food there," he replied.
We ran to the courtyard where Innocent's mother had a large basin full of slices of cooked yam and a pot of steaming stew displayed. She gave us some.
"I come here every day for lunch," Innocent said.
"Do you eat yam every day?" I asked.
"No, she cooks different things," he replied.
We played around the courthouse until the end-of-break bell rang; then we ran back to the school compound as the other students had fallen in line and were about to march to their classes. We managed to sneak into the middle of the line and walked along with them to the classroom.
On the way home, a fight broke out between two girls. This was the first time I witnessed two girls fighting on the way home from school: Ngozi and Chioma confronted each other over Ugoji. All the girls knew what the issue was, but they would not tell us. We separated them and maintained peace until we got home.
When we went out to play at the square in the evening, I chatted with Ugoji.
"Why were Chioma and Ngozi fighting on our way home from school?"
"I borrowed Chioma's book in class, and Ngozi didn't like it," he explained.
"I am confused. Why did Ngozi get offended?" I asked.
"Ogbuleke, please let us play; I don't want to talk about it," he said.
On Saturday, when we gathered at the square for soccer practice, all eyes were on Chioma and Ngozi. Without any sign of anger or hatred, they laughed, giggled, and jumped rope together.
"Girls are strange. How could two people fight one day and become friends again the next day?" I thought.
"You should never get yourself involved with any girl," Ugoji said.
"Why are you involved with Chioma?"
"That's enough; let's play," he said.
On Monday morning, we were crossing the famous Igwu Bridge

The Courage To Aspire

when Chioma whispered in Ngozi's ears, and both of them broke out laughing. Ugoji looked at me as if to remind me what he had told me at the square about girls. When we got to school, I went to clean Miss Kanu's backyard, and Chioma was there talking to Oyidiya. Both of them were laughing hysterically. I believed they were talking about Ugoji.

"What are you laughing about?" I asked.

"I can't tell you; it's something girls like to talk about," she said.

After the morning assembly, class started with arithmetic, followed by the English language. During the lunch break, Innocent and I went to the courtyard, and his mother gave us akara. Then we returned to the school compound before the end of recess, lined up and marched to the classroom.

On Saturday, Mom and Dad woke up before everybody else. They chatted for a while before Mom went to the kitchen. It was about the strategy for the day's farm work. Mom had some ideas about what to do before the sun started to pump heat waves down to Earth and who should be doing what.

Mom's preferred plan was that both of them should rake the soil, side by side until they had covered the whole lot. Then they would plant the yams, side by side, until the end of the day or until both of them got tired. However, Dad wanted to till the ground while Mom planted the yams after him.

"If we tilled the whole lot, any one of us could come back and finish planting the yams, with or without the other," she said. "But if I trail behind planting yams after you, then both of us have to come back together to continue in that manner. Tilling and planting by one person do not look too good either."

"OK, you're right. Let's get ready. I think we can finish everything today," Dad responded, patting Mom on the shoulder.

Mom prepared pepper soup with ginger and some other herbs; then we left the house before anybody else was up. When we got to the farm, Dad made a shed for Anyele and me, Mom prepared a fireplace for cooking, and then both of them attacked the land. They tilled the ground forward and sideways until they had covered the plot.

"Get some rest while I cook some food," Mom advised.

Chuks I. Ndukwe

"I want to walk down to the stream and take a quick bath," Dad replied.

"Nooo, it will make you lazy," she said.

"OK, give me water," he said.

"Here, give it to your dad and get some firewood," she said.

Mom cooked yams and served them with the vegetable sauce she had made at home. After lunch, she gave Anyele a bath before they went back to work.

At the end of the day, as the sun was receding into the west over the colorful horizon, we packed up and then took a long bath in the river.

On Monday morning, Mr. Nwabeze mounted a notice board beside the blackboard.

"This board is the class merit board," he announced. "We will have tests and quizzes every Friday. On Monday morning, three names will appear on this board; those three names will represent the students who came first, second, and third. I look forward to seeing your name on this board."

We'd had a merit board before, so it wasn't a surprise or a big deal, for that matter. I turned around to see Elendu Iheke and Elechi Uche's facial expressions; they were looking at me too, so I turned away quickly. With the battle joined, and the old rivalry renewed the competition began. During the Easter break, Mr. Nwabeze took me home to spend the break with his family. On our way, I saw a big, long thing moving along in the bush with smoke coming out of it; then it blew a loud horn. I was struggling to ask what it was when Mr. Nwabeze began to explain what it was.

"That is called 'train,' " he said.

"Why is smoke coming out of it?"

"It's burning coal; they use it to make steam to drive the train," he explained.

That was too complicated for me, so I did not ask any more questions, but the whole place had a strange smell.

When we got to his house, he introduced me to his family members. His sister, Elizabeth—who was about twelve years old—led me to a room at the backyard, and wanted me to call her Liz.

The Courage To Aspire

"What is the meaning of Liz?" I asked.

"It is the short form of Elizabeth," she explained.

"OK, what is the meaning of Elizabeth?"

"She is the queen of England."

"What do you mean by that?" I asked.

She walked out, leaving me alone until her mother came and got me.

"Take your bath and join us for dinner," she said.

I took a bath and joined them for dinner. Liz and I did not make eye contact. I thought she hated me for asking all those questions, but I knew she was wrong. My name means "a warrior who killed his enemy on Eke market day," Why shouldn't I know the meaning of her name too? Maybe in Ovim, people's names do not have meanings. For two days, she avoided me, and I followed her mother around—helping her in the kitchen and with garden work.

"You are so helpful," she said.

"I help my mom, too," said I.

Surprisingly, she did Mom's head-rubbing routine and smiled. I don't know why people liked to rub my head.

"Take Ogbuleke to the train station and show him around," she said to Liz.

On our way to the station, she seemed uncomfortable; she tried to look at me, and then she looked away.

"When we get to the station, don't ask me questions," she said. "Let me just show you around and tell you about the whole station, OK?"

"Yes," I promised.

When we got to the station, she showed me the platform, the waiting room, and the ticket window. People were buying tickets, and then we heard the horn and saw smoke rising far away.

"Look over there. The train is coming; stand by me," Liz said, grabbing my hand.

The long train with a black engine rolled into the station with a loud noise and stopped. Many people came down from the train, and many people got on the train.

"These people are coming home, and those who got into the train are going away," she explained.

It was exciting. Mr. Nwabeze's town was far better than mine. Liz and I became friends again.

The following day, Mr. Nwabeze took me to the Methodist bookstore.

"This is where all the Methodist schools get their textbooks from," he said.

He bought pencils, a ruler, and a notebook for me. After that, we stopped at a small market, where he bought some biscuits for me. I ate some and saved some for Liz.

We attended church on Sunday, and we returned home in the evening. The visit turned out to be a bittersweet experience because when kids in my class heard about it, I became the most disliked kid in the class. Whenever I got close to anyone of my classmates, he or she would simply walk away as if I had committed a crime.

I decided to spend a lunch break at Miss Kanu's residence with Oyidiya. One day, as I was walking to the teachers' quarters, Innocent called out "Ogbuleke stop," he ran and met me halfway to the teachers' quarters.

"Why are you avoiding me?" he asked. "I didn't do anything to you." He said.

"Everybody hates me. I thought you are one of those who hate me." I replied.

"No, I am not," he said. "I don't care if they hate me too," he said. "We're friends, and you did not do anything wrong. Let's go over to the courtyard."

We ran over to the courtyard, and his mother served us rice and goat meat.

A few weeks later, we began to prepare for the midyear examination. Innocent and I studied together whenever we had the chance. When the results of the tests came out, Innocent, and I had passed.

My anger for the treatment by my classmates without justifiable reason deepened. I studied every day with Innocent whenever possible, and week after week, I dominated the performance board with resolute determination to outperform in the final exam.

The Courage To Aspire

In November, as the weather started to change, chilly air blew over the town, bringing fog with it and hazy sunshine, reminding everybody the end of the year was around the corner.

One morning the headmaster announced, "The final examination will start in two weeks. Behave yourselves, and make this school proud."

Two weeks later, Mr. Nwabeze, Mr. Eleke, and Miss Kanu were gone, and three teachers from different schools took their places. The exam lasted for a week. The headmaster and his wife walked around every classroom, observing, supervising, and taking notes while other teachers conducted the examination. On the last day of school, the bell rang, and without lining up or marching, we gathered in the assembly hall. After the prayer, every teacher announced the results for his or her class.

Innocent was squeezing my hand when Mr. Nwabeze read the results for our class. When he heard his name, he took off running, and then he came back. I came; first, Innocent came second, and Elechi came third. At the end of the assembly, the headmaster stepped forward again and congratulated everybody who had passed the exam.

"Alayi Methodist Central School outperformed every school in our division. You made the teaching staff proud. Enjoy your holidays," he concluded.

Innocent and I hugged, and then he took off again running to give his mother the good news. Mr. Nwabeze walked up to me and shook my hand.

"My mother would love to know you did well on the final," he said.

Ugoji, Oyidiya, and I went to Miss Kanu's residence to celebrate with orange Fanta and biscuits. Also, We helped Miss Kanu pack while Oyidiya prepared rice and stew. When we finished packing, we ate; then Miss Kanu locked her residence, and then we went home.

When I got home, Ejere Igwe—my best friend—was waiting for me at the square.

"Where did you go?" he asked.

"I went to Miss Kanu's house," I replied.

We spent some time with Mom before we went over to his house.

Chuks I. Ndukwe

We spent the afternoon together—shooting down mangoes.
    Mom's stomach had become big again; she would place my hand on her belly to feel the baby's movement. One day, on my way from school, I heard a gunshot. (Fathers celebrated their children's delivery with a gunshot.) When I got home, women were dancing in the compound, and men were celebrating with palm wine. "Your mother has given birth to a baby girl," Dad said. "Her name is Nwakaego—meaning more precious than money. Go and see her in the bedroom." When I saw Mom smiling—she looked so happy and beautiful—it made me happy too.

Chapter 6
Sweet Reunion

Sometimes it's easy to forget how much you miss people until you see them again.

~ Colleen Hoover

It was quite an unexpected turn of events when the novelty of coming first in class—accompanied by my parents' excitement over performance in school—evaporated. Coming first in class became unimportant, and I found myself running away from Mom to avoid her hugs and praises and stayed away from her until Dad sent for me.

Lost in a state of stubbornness where my brain and mind locked in the jaws of a wrench, I decided there was not going to be any more celebration and obsession about coming first in the class had to end. I realized the only thing that mattered was the promotion—a fitting reward for passing the exam.

When I got home after hearing the results of the final exam, dinner was about to be served. Nwakaego was crying. Her voice rising to its highest pitch as she resisted any attempt to be touched. I stretched out my hands, beckoning her to climb on me, as she loved to do. As I picked her up, her heartbeat began to regulate, and that high-pitched voice modulated into cadenced murmuring.

"I will never stay away that long again," I said, patting her on the back.

I settled her in my laps, held her with one hand and fed her with the other. Mom sat still, watching us; she looked like she was about to cry.

"Let me take her so you can eat," she said.

"No, I will eat when she is full."

A few minutes later, she started spitting out the food, a signal that she didn't want anymore. Then I handed her back to Mom, and then I ate my food.

Chuks I. Ndukwe

Throughout the night, the final exam never came up for discussion, nor did anybody ask any question about the last day of school. I went to bed, gratified that my wish had come true. The cold, skin-cracking wind blew through the opening in the roof. Moonlight penetrated the room with a cold radiance to rival the light of our wick lamp, while the glowing embers in the fireplace tinted the walls and furniture with exotic colors.

✸✸✸

One Saturday morning, a rumor flew around like wildfire.
"Egbichi is coming home for Christmas," Mama Anya said.
"She is coming home to stay permanently," her sister said.
"Papa Nwanochie is coming home," Mom said.
"Okoro Onwuchekwa is coming home for Christmas," his brother said.

A few days later, people began to stream past the square in the morning to the motor park to wait for their relatives who were coming home for Christmas. In the evenings, they streamed past in the opposite direction carrying their luggage. On Saturday morning, a few people from the village traveled to Ovim to wait for Okoro Onwuchekwa at the train station. The next day Anyele and I went to greet him. When we got to his house, his father told us he did not make it because he had missed his train.

Late in the evening, while we gathered at the square, a large group of people from the motor park arrived at the same time carrying trunks and bags, and one person was pushing a bicycle. Unexpectedly, somebody grabbed me from the back and covered my eyes. I had no chance of seeing all the people who were in the crowd so I did not know who was blindfolding me.

"Guess who this is," the voice asked.

I rubbed the hand. Obviously, it was a girl's hand, and the only girl close enough to grab me like that was Oyidiya. "No, that is not her voice."

"Egbichi," I said.

I turned around as she let go, and we locked up in a protracted hug.

The Courage To Aspire

Then she took my hand.

"Let's go home. Oh, look at Anyele; he's grown," she said, hugging Anyele.

As we passed our house on our way to her home, she ran straight to Mom and embraced her. She picked Nwakaego up and brought her along. We kept looking at each other. "Now she looks pretty—nothing like my old playmate," I thought. We smiled and kept walking.

When we got to her house, Mama Anya was outside waiting for Egbichi. When she saw us entering their compound, she dashed forward and stretched out her long arms, hugging all of us together. We followed her to the house.

Egbichi gave her sister bread and biscuits to give to people who came to greet her.

"Don't worry about Ogbuleke and his brother and sister," she said.

"Come on; take your bath. The water is getting cold," Mama Anya said.

When Egbichi finished bathing, she called out. "Ogbuleke, bring me a towel."

"Let me take it to her," Mama Anya said.

Egbichi changed her clothes and sat by my side. "I packed a box for you; after dinner, we will take it to your house," she said.

After dinner, we went to our house, and Mom and Dad were eating dinner. I was not surprised they had not come to get us; they knew Mama Anya would take good care of us. Egbichi shook Anyele. "Look at you! You were a baby when I left," she said.

When Mom and Dad finished eating, Egbichi opened the box. She gave Mom crayfish and stock-fish, she gave Anyele a T-shirt, and she gave me a pair of black shorts and a white shirt. Then she gave us two loaves of bread and some biscuits.

"I don't have anything for the baby; I didn't know about her," she said. "Father Ikebie, I don't have anything for you either. I am sorry."

"My dear, you've given me more than you can imagine," Dad said.

The next day music was blaring everywhere in the village; Papa Nwanochie and Okoro Onwuchekwa had come home with a gramophone. They played all kinds of records, and kids danced and played with delight.

Chuks I. Ndukwe

With Egbichi at home, the desire for playing in the square with my mates diminished. We hung around together, reminiscing and telling each other everything we missed. As always, we busted out laughing and giggling every now and then. Something had happened, though, but it was not readily apparent. We did not jump into the sand to play our usual games, and we did not grab and climb on each other, as we had previously loved to do. Instead, we ran around together, holding hands. Sometimes, with one hand over the other's shoulder and the other hand around the waist, we walked together as if the world belonged to us. Nobody was surprised, nor should they; we were acting and behaving the same way as we used to do before she went away.

On Sunday after church service, I had just finished changing my clothes when Egbichi crashed through the door.

"We can't call each other by our names; I don't like it anymore," she said.

"If not, then what?" I asked

"We should call each other friend," she said.

"OK," I said, not really grasping the reason for that suggestion.

How she came up with that idea, I did not know or care. She went to the kitchen to talk to Mom before leaving.

"Friend, I will be back," she said, sprinting out of the compound.

In the evening, elders gathered around the burning fire in every compound as the cold weather lingered like an unwelcome visitor.

"Go and tell your mother that we will eat by the burning fire," Dad said.

I ran and told Mom—eating outside was fun.

"Take water with you. The food is ready; come back and take some plates," Mom said.

The whole compound ate outside by the burning fire. After dinner, we lay around until bedtime, absorbing the gentle heat emanating from the radiance of the blazing fire.

On Monday, we went to the farm. Surprisingly, Mama Anya's lot was next to ours, and they came to the farm too. It was like a reunion on the farm. Egbichi and I helped watch Nwakaego. We carried her to the stream and bathed her whenever we felt the heat was too high for her to cope with.

The Courage To Aspire

At the stream, Egbichi took her clothes off and walked straight to me.

"Friend, look," she said. "I am growing hair on my thing, and my breasts are sticking out too. That is why we can't play like we used to. I am a woman now."

I was shocked and speechless. Egbichi seemed to know everything, and I knew nothing. I rubbed my chest; it was as flat as ever. I looked at my thing, and there was no hair on it. I was confused and somewhat ashamed because I felt like Egbichi had gotten smarter and had everything—hair and breasts I did not have.

"How can you have hair on your thing while I have none?" I asked. "We were born at the same time. Let me touch your hair, and you can touch mine."

She took my hand and placed it on her thing.

"Do you feel it?" she asked.

"Yes, I do; feel mine," I said.

"You are right; you have no hair on it," she said, laughing and giggling like the good old days.

"OK, if you are a woman now, what am I?" Feeling embarrassed.

"Let's go and ask your mother. We cannot let Father Ikebie know. I am afraid of him," she said.

We asked Mom why Egbichi was growing hair, her breasts were sticking out, and I had nothing growing on my body.

"That's natural; girls develop faster than boys," Mom explained, "and boys don't grow breast."

At the end of the day, we went down to the riverside. Men and women separated into two groups, with men up-river and women down-river as villagers called both places. As I had observed before, women covered their lower front and back, while men walked unabashed into the water with their things dangling around.

"Why do women cover their thing?"

"Nobody is supposed to see their thing. You can't see mine anymore."

"Why?" I asked.

"Because it is a holy place," she said.

From that day on, everything changed. I tried not to go near her at

Chuks I. Ndukwe

all.

I avoided her for a week, but then I began to miss her, so I went over to her house.

"You've been busy playing soccer and forgot that I exist," she snapped.

"I am sorry. I don't know how to talk to you now that you are a woman. Boys don't like talking to women," I stammered.

"We can still do everything, but you can't see or touch my body," she said.

We hung out together for a while; then Kanu came for me, so I left. Later in the evening, Mom sent for Egbichi to eat dinner with us. When I got to her house, she had just finished grinding egusi for her mother.

"Sit down," she said.

I sat down. And then Egbichi sat on my laps.

"See, nothing changed. Maa, I told my friend that he can't see or touch my body anymore. Am I right or wrong?" she asked.

"She is right; she is a young woman now," her mother concurred.

"Mom wants you to come over for dinner," I told her.

"OK, let's go. Maa, don't wait for me," she told her mother.

On the way to our house, we held hands and walked side by side as if I had forgotten all the lectures about her woman's body.

After dinner, she played with Nwakaego and gave her a bedtime bath. Then she left.

"I still remember when the two of you were little babies," Mom said. "Mama Anya and I would sit both of you down side by side, and you'd be throwing sand at each other's face. Now look at both of you—still arguing about every little thing and yet clinging to each other like a fly on honey."

If Egbichi were a boy, we would be fighting every day because of the weird dynamics between us; she liked to get her way with me, and I'd resist most of the time.

On the day Okoro Onwuchekwa left, I went to Egbichi's house to find out if she was planning to leave too.

"When are you leaving?" I asked.

"Who told you I was leaving?" Egbichi asked in return.

"You don't answer a question with a question."

The Courage To Aspire

"Too bad, I will. Who told you?" She asked again.
"Nobody told me I just want to know."
"I am not leaving. You should be happy that I am back."
"Just so you know, I am not; I'm not sure you'll not vanish again."
"Are you angry because I did not tell you before I left the first time?" She asked. "Friend, I am not leaving like that ever again."

The next Sunday, I went to church with Ugoji and Oyidiya. Miss Kanu was not in the church that day, and it was unusual for her not to attend church.

"How about Miss Kanu, what happened to her?" I asked.
"She went to Ovim," Ugoji said.

Later in the afternoon, Egbichi came over.
"Let's go over to my house. My mother cooked a Sunday meal for us," she said.

When we got to her house, her mother served dinner with orange Fanta.

On Monday morning, school kids defied the cold weather and ran to the stream, dived into the water, and took a bath in the cold water. On our way home from the stream, our teeth clattered, and our bodies shivered as we ran to the burning fire to warm up. In every home, mothers had kernel oil ready to rub over their children's young bodies to protect them from cracking and turning ashy.

The Methodist School senior building contained standard five and six classrooms—a traditional building with doors and windows; other buildings were open halls with walls halfway to the ceiling. Sitting in that classroom, I could not help but feel an air of pride and superiority, and self-awareness as a senior student.

During the lunch break, we roamed around the school and the court surroundings. Then after lunch, we played with crumpled-up pieces of paper. We threw them around the classroom at random sparing nobody. Launchers hit back with shots as well, and every successful hit cheered loudly until my teacher showed up.

The following morning, seniors went to Ovim to buy their school materials. At dinner, I reminded Mom to wash my uniform.

On Monday after the morning assembly, we walked to our classroom and took our seats. Then Mrs. Okocha came in the class with a long, thin metallic pole —her staff.

"We will start class every day with roll call," she said. "Your names are in alphabetical order. When I call your name, I want you to say 'here' or 'present.' If I do not hear your answer, you will be marked absent. If you come to class after the roll call, you will be punished, so try to be in class before the roll call, both in the morning and after the lunch break."

The seating order was exactly the same as it had always been, small or short kids in front and big or tall ones at the back—a natural order perhaps, so this year was no different.

After the roll call, senior students came in the classroom and distributed the books and other essential materials they had bought at the Methodist bookstore for us. The books smelled so good; we had a notebook for every subject. Every day, we went home with textbooks and notebooks for the next topic.

Everything was different in standard five. We did lots of reading and writing. Occasionally, we wrote letters to our parents, brothers, sisters, and our teacher—and sometimes a formal or official letter to whatever office the teacher chose for us. Arithmetic had gotten harder, and English-language classes covered grammar, précis, and composition. Mrs. Okocha gave us many assignments too. We studied problems in advance before she went to the blackboard to make short presentations; then she left us to figure things out.

Mrs. Okocha treated us very differently from students in the lower classes. We did not have to leave the classroom during lunch, and occasionally, we worked on problems or assignments during lunch. Mrs. Okocha did not conduct weekly tests, nor did she have a weekly merit board on which to post the names of students who were leading academically. Instead, she conducted impromptu tests at any time of her choosing. She did not disclose the result of the tests; instead, she counseled students who did not meet what she called "her expectation." She did not talk to students who did well in the tests.

At home, elders were calling on me to write letters for them when they needed to communicate with their relatives who lived abroad. The provincial chief, Anyele Ochu, sent for me every week—especially on Sundays—to come over and write a letter for one of his children. He

The Courage To Aspire

dictated his thoughts, and I put them in writing. Then he gave me money to buy stamps and mail the letter. Every time I wrote a letter for the chief, he gave me dried meat; he always had the most delicious dried meat in stock. He would tell stories about the colonial days—how the white people had come, established the court system, and made him a ruler in our town.

On Sunday, a week before the midyear examination, Mr. and Mrs. Okocha attended church at Amankalu Methodist Church. After church, they accompanied Uncle Okereke and Azik to our house. Dad served his Sunday delight —undiluted palm wine, while Mom cooked her Sunday special. I was there to tend to them, sometimes nervous and sometimes loose enough to smile.

Before they left, Mrs. Okocha chatted with Mom. "Would you let Ikebie stay with my relatives Mathew and Lydia at the teachers' quarters during the break?" she asked. "My husband and I are going away for the week."

"Let me consult with his father," Mom replied.

After brief discussions with Dad, she said it was OK.

While we were descending the Igwu sloppy hill, Mrs. Okocha told me I would be spending the break with her relatives, Mathew and Lydia, at their school residence.

"Don't forget to bring some casual clothes to school on the last Friday before the break," she said.

"Yes, ma'am, I will not forget," I replied.

When we got to Igwu Bridge, she carried Nwakaego on her shoulder, chatted with Mom for a while, and then she patted me on the head and said, "Bye."

On our way home, I carried the Plump Face. That is what I had nicknamed Nwakaego because her fat cheeks which were a delight to pinch.

"Do you know that every teacher you've had invited you over to their residence or took you home to visit their families?" Mom asked.

"Yes, they like me because of Uncle Okereke,"

"Uncle Okereke doesn't even know most of those teachers," she said.

"OK, I am the smallest student in their classes."

"I bet you are not the smallest kid in those classes," she speculated.

During the week of the midyear examination, I was a nervous wreck. "I better not disappoint Mrs. Okocha," I kept thinking.

For every subject, I was the last person to leave the classroom. Some students finished in half the time allotted for the test. In most cases, I finished at the same time, other students did, but for whatever reason, I kept going over my papers until Mrs. Okocha practically snatched them from my hand.

"Ikebie, time is up," she would say.

Then I would stroll to her desk and hand my paper to her.

"Good job, Ikebie," she always said.

On the last Friday before the midterm break, the exam results were posted on the notice board; it was a pass/fail exam by tradition. I passed the exam.

After the closing assembly, Mrs. Okocha held my hand as we walked to her house. I remembered how my classmates had shunned me when I spent the holidays with Mr. Nwabeze's family. So I almost died when Mrs. Helen Okocha held my hand while walking to her residence.

✷✷✷

One morning—six months later—we had a combined assembly at the junior soccer field, and after the meeting, the headmaster made the following announcement:

"Final exam is upon us once again," he said. "A few teachers will be going away to conduct exams in various schools, and we will be hosting teachers from those schools to conduct your exam. Study hard and come back on Monday prepared."

During the week of the exam, classes started early, and students went home when they finished their last test for the day. For every subject, I was the last kid to turn in his paper; in some cases, the teacher had to remind me that time was up. I tried but failed to convince myself that my answers were correct. After each subject, my stomach churned and turned like a big wave crashing at the river's edge. I felt that way for at least three days after the end of the examination week.

Once the exam was over, we did whatever we wanted. On the last

The Courage To Aspire

day of the school year, the bell went off very early, and we assembled in the standard-four hall. Mrs. Okocha conducted the morning devotion. Then after the prayer, each teacher announced the result of his or her class examination in the order of merit. In my class, Elechi Uche took the first place, I came second, and Elendu Iheke came third. Students who did not hear their names failed the examination.

"We are closing the school early so that those of you who are traveling abroad to spend your holidays with your relatives can get to the motor park on time. Enjoy your holidays," the headmaster said.

I went home with Ejere Igwe after stopping briefly at Amokwelu Motor Park. When we got to our house, it was too early for lunch, so we continued on to his home and went fishing.

Chapter 7
The Best Christmas Ever

It's quite the family reunion we're having in here.

~ Cynthia Hand Boundless

Anyele and Nwakaego were lying in a straight line in the sand, facing in opposite directions, with their heads touching each other and their eyes locked in an unflinching stare at the sky—like fixtures of nature incapable of movement by their own volition. I stood from a distance and watched to see how and when they'd separate from each other. "What will be the cause?" I wondered. Something must be wrong; children that young are incapable of immersing themselves in such a state of abject oblivion, unaffected by the skin-cracking, cold wind that had put the village in a deep freeze and as I rushed over to shake them, they broke out giggling as if to say gotcha! They looked at me, turned around, and resumed their childish game. I found it amusing, but without bothering them, I went inside the house, where Mom was preparing lunch.

"You are home right on time," she said.

"What are those kids doing?"

"I have no idea," Mom said. They've been lying like that for a while. Then they changed position and continue; don't disturb them," Mom said.

I changed my clothes and returned to the kitchen to help her.

"Look, they are coming inside the house," Mom said.

They walked inside the house, covered with sand.

"Go ahead and eat. I've got to give these kids a bath before they eat," she said.

I wasn't used to eating alone, so I waited until she finished bathing them and then she wanted to know about the final examination.

The Courage To Aspire

"Did you pass?" she asked.
"Yes, I passed. I will be in standard six next year."
"That is very good. Are you happy?" Mom asked.
"Yes, I am a happy senior."

Later in the afternoon, I went over to Egbichi's house and spent the evening there.

"Brother Mba had sent a message that he's coming home for Christmas," she said.

"When is he coming home?"

"I don't know; my sister knows the date," she replied.

We waited for her sister, Ugo, to come home and tell us the date her brother was coming home, but she didn't get home before dinner, so I left. The wind blew fiercely over the thatched roof; the muffled sound of the wind gusts reaching everywhere in the village as the wind whistled sharply under the bamboo doors. Frightened animals in the stalls made fearful sounds of protest as the skin-cracking gusts blew against them. The phenomenon was scary with the wind blowing in my face, forcing my eyes to tear up. I got home and found Anyele, Nwakaego, and Dad bunched up and sleeping.

While they were sleeping, Uncle Anyele, the driver, arrived and informed Mom that my older brother, Dick, was coming home for Christmas. I have only heard about him as a footnote in a fairy tale, as he had been living in Aba with Uncle Emeke since he was a little boy, and had not come home since then. Mom was overwhelmed with joy; she paced around the house. "Finally, we will celebrate like other families," she said.

"When is he coming home?"

"We will find out by Sunday," she said.

Of course, I couldn't keep the secret hearing such exciting news; I ran over to Egbichi's house to tell her, stumbled a couple of times and learned Ugo was making plans to go to the motor park on the following Saturday.

"I am going to wait for your brother, Dick and brother Mba on Saturday," she said.

"Are they coming home together?" I asked.

"Yes, they are," she answered.

"OK, bye." I took off to go and tell Mom.

There we were, Mom, me and everybody else, all overcome by excitement. Mom began to prepare to go to the market to buy individual items to cook for Brother Dick on his arrival.

"Maa, he is coming home on Saturday," I said, screaming and jumping up and down, unable to control myself.

"Who told you?" she asked.

"Sister Ugo told me. She is going to the motor park on Saturday to wait for them. I want to go with her," I said.

Mom took off for the market with Mama Anya, both displaying a rare public emotion and happiness.

Mom brought home a big white fowl—a mature male chicken—a fat, dried portion of grass-cutter, fish, and a large slab of steak. She turned around, went back out to the farm, and returned with lots of cassava with which she made enough gari to last throughout my brother's visit.

Dad woke up, then Mom broke the news to him.

"It will be good to spend a warm Christmas in this house for a change," he said.

"Where will he sleep?" she asked.

"In Ogba Ochu's house," Dad replied.

"That's good enough," she said.

I suppose it's fair to say it does not take elaborate plans to accommodate a visiting relative.

On Saturday, Sister Ugo, Egbichi, and I went to the motor park. We arrived, hardly finding a space to stand, as the park was packed with people waiting for their relatives. Some people we knew came over to where we were standing.

"Who are you waiting for?" they asked.

"We are waiting for brother Mba and Dick; they are returning together," Ugo said.

"Oh yes, Father Ikebie's son—I haven't seen him since he was little," she said.

Talking as she was and not getting the audience she deserved, a bus comes gliding down the Igbere-Alayi hill. People rushed to take positions to give them easy access to the bus conductor. As the bus

The Courage To Aspire

began to crawl up the sloppy Amokwelu hill, pandemonium ensued. The conductor ran behind the bus carrying a wooden wedge on his shoulder.

The bus stopped, and people began to jump in—after paying the fare—while their luggage piled up by the vehicle, only to be loaded after the bus had been filled. Suddenly the conductor closed the doors, and the driver, aided by the conductor, shoved luggage into the opening under the bus until all the bags had disappeared. The conductor removes the wedge from under the bus and puts the wedge on his shoulder, and then the bus rolled down the hill until it disappeared from sight.

We realized how screwed: we had come to the park rather too early, but couldn't go home fearing brother Dick and Mba could arrive any time. I remember strolling around the park eating some yams with tomato stew and drinking orange Fanta.

We roamed around till late in the afternoon, and then vehicles began to arrive from the opposite direction all eyes on the court clerk's residence which provides the first glimpse of any object struggling to get up the hill from Ezialayi valley. Eyes straining and anticipation at its pitch, the first vehicle crosses the courtyard; the famous Peugeot 404 driven by Uncle Anyaele. It arrived and passed without making a stop. Suddenly a procession of vehicles began to arrive at random intervals. A truck labeled "Chikezie" arrived and unloaded its passengers, and "Amokwe Item Express" stopped and dropped off its load. I remember "Ogadimma" crawling up the hill and stopping. It did not grab our attention at first until Egbichi screamed.

"I can see them in that lorry."

"I can see Brother Dick," Ugo shouted.

There they are my brother, Dick, and Brother Mba getting off the lorry and both equally handsome and attractive. I had met Mba before, so it was easy to determine who my brother was.

Both spent a long time hugging the girls before giving me any attention, to my uttermost disgust.

In the beginning, I'm guessing he didn't realize I've been waiting all my life—ten years—to see him but I'm sure in a few minutes everything would change.

Suddenly he turned around, picked me up, and swung me round

and round, just as I do Anyele. As he was swinging me around, my anger evaporated.

As we hung around, waiting for their luggage to be unloaded the lure of the park, happy faces, waiting for their loved ones, and the aroma of all kinds of confectionaries became overwhelming.

Once the luggage was all sorted out, we left the park. Egbichi and I carried Brother Dick's belongings, and Ugo Brother Mba's.

Mom was restlessly waiting to see Brother Dick, and immediately we entered our compound, Mom and Brother Dick locked themselves up in a warm embrace while Anyele and Nwakaego looked on. Mom picked Nwakaego up and handed her over to Dick.

'What is her name?" he asked.

"Nwaka, same as mine," she answered.

Dad came out with arms spread, and they too engaged in another long embrace.

"Welcome home, Son," Dad said.

All that time, I was staring at the luggage, eager to start opening it to see what he had brought home with him. He was still standing outside, talking to Mom when people began to come in groups to greet him.

"Come on. Take your bath," Mom said.

"Let me give Ogbuleke his gift," he said.

He gave me two white shirts, two pairs of black shorts, one singlet, and two polo shirts. Anyele got two shirts and a couple of shorts, and Nwakaego got three little blouses. As for Mom and Dad, they got different things, not that they cared for the gift. I suppose now, just thinking about it, all they wanted was to see their black, tall, and handsome son.

At dinner, Mom served the best meal she'd ever cooked, and Dick enjoyed the meal so much he fell asleep shortly after.

One thing that stuck in my mind is what happened the next day as a group of boys were playing soccer at the square. Suddenly Dick and Mba emerged dressed in a black and white suit and bright red tie looking as handsome as ever—on their way to visit some girl. I had not thought about it until that moment, I rushed home, and Dad was sitting in his usual corner grinning with joy probably visualizing his son. No

The Courage To Aspire

wonder he always referred to him as "Handsome Man." I was very proud of him.

As rumor had it, they had gone to a village called Umuezike. I waited all evening for him to come home. By that time, I was conflicted by the desire to spend as much time with him as possible and his right to visit the girl if it made him happy. He stayed late, way past dinnertime, and neither Mom nor Dad was angry. He came home feeling more pleased than he was before he left.

On Sunday, we had a surprise visitor: an elegant, beautiful girl. Mom wasn't happy to see that girl, and it showed on her face. Dad was visibly angry and wanted that visit to be the first and the last.

"Whatever is going on between both of you, I want it to stop," Dad said.

"You will like her and her family when you get to learn about them," Dick said.

"You will regret it if you continue to chase after her—mark my words," Dad replied.

Here came Mba as the discussion was reaching its boiling point.

"Mba, what do you say about that girl?" Dad asked.

"I wouldn't pursue that girl; I told Brother Dick already," he answered.

All those remarks and responses sounded like a Ping-Pong ball clearing the net with each backhand strike and flying back to the opposition with a counterstroke. After that exchange, Dick and Mba left together, and I did not see them until the next morning when we sat down for breakfast.

"Ogbu, how are you doing in school?" Dick asked.

"I am doing well. I will be in standard six when school reopens."

"When you finish standard six, you can come and live with me," he said.

I was thrilled to hear that—but what I really wanted was to spend as much time with him as possible.

Late in the afternoon, both of them came home riding the chrome bicycle. For weeks, they went everywhere on that bicycle. On some days, they left in the morning and came home after dinner. I did not see much of him until Christmas Day; his homecoming seemed so different.

Chuks I. Ndukwe

I spent the Christmas Eve with Mama Ugo Okereke; in the evening we attended choir practice together—she was like a second mother to me. She did not have a child of her own, so I spent as much time as I could with her, and I did things that I could not do with Mom with her—such as going to church and singing in the choir.

On that day, we rehearsed all Harcourt White's songs, and at the end of the practice, the leader chose songs for the Christmas celebration. I returned home singing those songs in my mind all night, looking at the string of light that pierced through an opening in the roof hoping night would fly rather than crawl.

Early on Christmas Day, I went to the stream and bathed. I hummed the songs while in the water and on the way home. Then I went to Mama Ugo's house, she served breakfast, and then we went to church hand in hand.

The church was overflowing, leaving a large number of attendees outside the church building. There were many new faces in the congregation. I presumed many of them were people who had returned home to celebrate Christmas with their families, and others were probably those who attended church only on Christmas Day. The elders were in their chairs, the catechist in his high place, and Uncle Okereke sat beside him. The choir brought the church attendees to their feet as we sang Harcourt White's songs. The catechist preached the Gospel making the service a grand, joyful occasion.

When the service ended, Mama Ugo invited me to her house, but I wanted to go home and sit between Anyele and Nwakaego and put my hands around them and rock them sideways until they tried to run away from me as they always did. I left the church, sprinting home nonstop. I sat between Anyele and Nwakego and rocked them while I sang Christmas songs. Many people visited our house for the Christmas celebration.

Two weeks later, brother Dick's visit ended. On Saturday morning, Egbichi, Sister Ugo, Mom, and I escorted brother Dick and Mba to Amokwelu Motor Park. When we got there, "Ohabike" was loading, and a few seats were still available. The lorry ran straight from Igbere to Aba, so my brother and Mba paid their fares and got on the truck, which was a pickup truck with a wooden enclosure and seats—without any

The Courage To Aspire

delay.

We waited for a few minutes, then the conductor removed his wedges, and Ohabike rolled away. The conductor jumped on the lorry, and everybody waved. We watched the truck until it went out of sight.

When we returned home, the unavoidable pain and anguish of separation from a loved one—even though it was temporary—brought everybody down to the point of near depression. Mom sobbed and covered her face; she did not want us to see her cry. I was surprised to see her sob like that because I expected her to be stronger; she was always calm and undisturbed by any situation.

On Monday, the first day of school, I felt completely different. The thought of being a senior at Alayi Methodist Central School gave me a sense of pride. The morning bell rang, and we lined up according to class and height and marched up and down the main walkway, and finally, we separated into two sidewalks resembling a gigantic letter "Y", leading to the two assembly halls. After the prayer, we marched to our classes. The headmaster walked into the classroom like the commander of the first battalion of the Nigerian armed forces.

"Class, stand, sit," he says. "Stand, sit. Good morning, class," he greeted us.

"Good morning, sir," we replied.

"Be seated. Who doesn't know who I am? Raise your hand."

No hand went up.

"That's good, I am the headmaster of this institution of learning, Alayi Methodist Central School," he says. "My job is to guide you, and your job is to study and learn. The only bad question is one that is not asked, so do not be afraid to ask about anything that is on your mind. I want you to feel free and comfortable."

"We will go round the class beginning with Ikebie. Stand up and tell the class your name and where you are from."

"My name is Ogbuleke Ikebie, and I am from Amaigwu Amankalu Alayi," I said.

"We will applaud at the end of the introductions. Next," Mr. Okocha said.

We continued the introduction until the last student spoke. Then we applauded.

"I will conduct a roll call at the beginning of the class every morning and after lunch break every afternoon. Make sure that you are in the class and seated before the roll call starts," Mr. Okocha said "Coming in while the roll call is in progress will earn you, a mild punishment and walking into the class after the roll call will put you in the doghouse. He does not like anybody in his house. Is that clear?"

"Yes, sir," we responded.

"Bring out your composition notebook, and write a summary of how you spent your last Christmas holidays," he said. "Put your notebook on my desk when you finish, facedown."

We placed our ink bottles in a little, round recessed spot on the desk, nibs fitted in their places, and then we began to write the summary. The writing was not easy or fun then. We had to dip the pen in the ink bottle; made sure the ink was not dripping down on the paper, and then carefully wrote on the paper with a blotter in the other hand to soak up the ink—should it act up. When we finished writing the summary, we placed our notebooks on the headmaster's desk, face down—as he instructed.

"You can pick up your notebooks after the lunch break," he said.

The next subject was reading, so he gave us a passage to learn from a book that I cannot remember any more. Throughout lunchtime, we read the passage holding the book on one hand and a ball of akara or maimai on the other.

"You are free to stay in the class or go outside during lunch break," he said, "but you must be in class before roll call to avoid punishment."

I had finished reading the passage, so I bought some maimai and ate it under the mango tree.

The bell went off; we lined up and marched into our classes, picking up our notebooks as we walked into the classroom past the headmaster's desk. Then we opened our notebooks and found comments from "redo," to "good," to "very good." He wrote, "Redo" in red, and other comments in black. If he gave you "redo" you had to rewrite the summary and hand it in before going home that day.

Chapter 8
A Moment Of Inspiration

What you are looking for is already in you...You already are everything you are seeking.

~ Thich Nhat Hanh.

One Monday morning, we started school with marching, morning devotion, and prayer before walking to our classrooms. The headmaster walked in and conducted his roll call.

"We will have a special visitor this afternoon. He is a scientist from America;" he said. "His team of engineers is here to conduct exploration. They will perform a demonstration for us here in this classroom, so come back before the afternoon roll call."

When you're a child, one of the most beautiful things about the notification is the restless embrace of immediacy, thereby pitching patience against the currency. In this case, immediacy and currency won so all through the lunch break, we waited restlessly to see the scientist; an American whose name we've only seen in the test book. In our young minds, scientists are not real people, let alone visit our school. There we were, lost in a zone of high anticipation, anxious to see and hear what the scientist from America had to say.

Suddenly, a car entered the school compound and went straight to the headmaster's residence. Two people got out of the car: a big, tall black man walked toward our classroom, followed by a white man of average height carrying a box.

As soon as he crossed the classroom entrance, the headmaster shouted. "All stand, Salute."

"Good afternoon, sir," we greeted.

"Good afternoon, class," he greeted back.

"Be seated," the headmaster ordered.

Chuks I. Ndukwe

"We have extraordinary visitors this afternoon. They are a group of scientists who will be spending a few weeks with us," the headmaster said. "They are conducting explorations to determine if we have any deposits of rare minerals in this division. I will let the scientist introduce himself and explain the demonstration he intends to perform this afternoon for us."

"My name is David Marshal," the black scientist said. "My companion, Henry Anderson, and I are electrical engineers. You must have seen the light that comes on every evening around the rest house at the end of the soccer field. It is called 'electric light. I've arranged for a wire to be run around the field, so one day before we depart, you will play a game under the electric light. Meanwhile, I will demonstrate how the light is generated. Observe so you can ask questions afterwards."

The white man opened the box and took out wires, screwdrivers, bulbs and switches, and a big battery. He put the battery on top of the table and connected the cables to the sockets and the switch. Then he joined the wire to the battery and inserted the bulbs into the sockets.

"I would like one of you to volunteer and come up; don't be afraid," he said.

Without giving the scientist time to finish the sentence, I was by his side already. I must confess jumping out of the seat and running to the front of the class at the request of my teacher without thinking about the reason was a typical behavior on my part. However, at that time my curiosity was in overdrive

"Thank you," he said. "This is what I want you to do. This is a switch, and that is a toggle. You can move it up or down; this direction is up, and the opposite direction is down. I want you to hold the toggle, and we will close all the windows and the door. When the classroom gets dark, I want you to move the toggle up."

Afraid of what might happen, I moved the toggle slowly upward, and light came on and illuminated the classroom. It was an unusual sight and amazing. I stared in disbelief. Then I screamed; "I want to become an electrical engineer when I grow up."

"You can go back to your seat. The light comes from the electric current stored in the battery," Mr. Marshal said. "Behind the rest house, a generator provides the current for the light you see around the rest

The Courage To Aspire

house."

Does anybody have any question for the scientist?" the headmaster asked.

"Yes, sir, I have three questions."

"Go ahead, Ikebie," the headmaster said.

"Can every electrical engineer make the light come on as you did?"

"Yes," he said.

"Does anybody else have a question?" the headmaster asked.

He waited for hands to go up, but none went up.

"OK, Ikebie, ask another question."

"Is every electrical engineer a scientist?" I asked.

"Yes."

"Ikebie, ask your last question," the headmaster said.

"What should I do to become an electrical engineer?"

"If you study math, advanced math, physics, English language, plus any other two subjects, and if you maintain a high enough grade, you can become an electrical engineer," he explained.

I jumped up again like a little possessed cat. "When I grow up, I want to become an electrical engineer!"

"Open the door and the windows," the headmaster said.

We opened the door and the windows.

"You can come up and take a look, one person at a time," the scientist said.

I ran up again, touching every piece of the setup thinking one day, I would be the engineer hooking up all those wires. Everybody in the class went up and looked at the setup closely. At the end of the demonstration, we stood up and gave the engineers loud applause. I remember the scientists leaving the classroom, and the class descending into deep silence; everybody seemed to be speechless or lost in amazement.

"Ikebie, why are you so excited about the experiment?" the headmaster asked.

"Sir, I want to become an electrical engineer."

"Who else wants to become an electrical engineer?" he asked.

I raised my hand up again, unable to contain myself.

"Not you, Ikebie. I mean other students."

Chuks I. Ndukwe

I wrote down a few things the scientist had said, notably that I could become an electrical engineer if I were good at math, advanced math, physics, English language, and two other subjects. I also wrote down that every electrical engineer is a scientist.

"Can I see your notebook?" the headmaster requested.

I surrendered my notebook. The headmaster went over the notes I had made, and he handed my notebook back to me. Every time the headmaster asked the class to write a composition on what we wanted to be when we grew up, I'd write pages describing the first time I saw electric light, and how exhilarated I felt watching Mr. David Marshal conduct his demonstration in my classroom. Besides, I would end the composition with forward-looking expectations of how proud I would feel to light up a dark room with electric light.

The desire gradually stuck in my mind to the point thinking about it made me happy. Sometimes I felt like my imagination was running wild, messing up my mind; other times I felt like I was secure in God's sacred place every innocent child's aspiration and hope is safe and destined for fulfillment. **The reality was that I had no chance of becoming an electrical engineer, and there was not any road map for reaching that goal. Yet, I refused to accept the perversity of the divergence between a child's desire and its reality.**

One Friday afternoon, the school began the weekly cleaning, and Mrs. Helen Okocha sent for me.

"Ikebie, could you go over to the headmaster's residence and see Lydia?" she asked.

I dropped my broom and ran over to the headmaster's house, and Mathew was standing in front of the house.

"I am here to see Lydia," I told him.

"She is in the backyard," he said.

I walked straight through the living room to the backyard as a privileged guest or maybe adopted family member.

"Ikebie, I want you to go to the stream with Mathew and fetch me drinking water; we are running low," she ordered.

"OK, let me get permission from the headmaster."

"Go ahead, but you don't have to," she said.

I ran back to the classroom and found the headmaster his head

The Courage To Aspire

buried in a newspaper, reading without looking up.

"Excuse me, sir; Lydia wants me to go to the stream with Mathew to fetch drinking water. Can I go?" I asked.

"Yes, Ikebie, you can go," he said, smiling and shaking his head.

I turned around to walk out of the classroom, then he called me back and gave me some money; I had no idea how much it was.

"Tell Mathew to buy some snacks for both of you," he said.

"Oh, thank you, sir," I said and sprinted out of the classroom.

Before we went to the stream, Mathew bought salted groundnut roasted in ash which we munched on all the way to the stream.

On our way back, Mathew asked, "Ikebie, what is a scientist?"

"He is an electrical engineer," I answered.

"How do you know?"

"He came to my class."

"OK, why do you want to be an electrical engineer?" he asked again.

"I want to make electrical light."

"The headmaster thinks that you are years ahead of your age."

"Oh, I didn't mean to offend him. I say things without thinking. What should I do?" I asked and silently blamed myself for displaying such a distasteful act of precocity.

"No, it's not bad. The headmaster says that you are brilliant," Mathew said.

Talking as we did, I did not feel the weight of the pail of water I was carrying, nor did the distance from the stream to the school seem any longer than the gap between our school and the soccer field. We got back on time, just before the final bell went off.

"Ikebie, would you like to go to Umuahia with us?" Lydia asked.

"Why?" I asked.

"To travel with us and visit Mama Rose."

"Who is Mama Rose?"

"She is Mr. Okocha's mother."

"She doesn't know me; I'd be shy to see her."

"Don't be silly. Mr. Okocha talks about you all the time, and his mother wants you to come and spend Easter break with her."

"I've to go now," I said and left.

Chuks I. Ndukwe

When I got to the classroom, the headmaster was still there sitting on his desk reading the newspaper.

"Sir, we are back."

"That's very good. See you on Monday," he said.

I picked up my lunch bag, my math textbook, and my notebook and joined my group, and went home. I did not tell Mom and Dad about what Lydia had told me because I did not give credence to it. Two weeks before the Easter break, Mrs. Okocha gave me a letter to give my parents. I rushed home and read the letter to Mom and Dad.

Dear Mr. and Mrs. Ndukwe,

My mother-in-law, Mrs. Rose Okocha, has asked us to invite your son Ogbuleke to visit her family in the town of Umuahia during the Easter holidays. Would you please do us the honor of allowing your son to travel to Umuahia with us on the last Friday before the beginning of the Easter holidays?

We are looking forward to a favorable reply.

Sincerely,
Helen M. Okocha

After hearing the letter, Mom and Dad sat in total silence. I handed the letter to Dad, and as I was about to run out of the house, he said, "Get your pen and paper."

"They are in school. I don't bring them home," I told Dad.

"Bring them home on Monday. We want to reply to that letter soon," he said.

On Monday, I brought my pen and ink bottle home, and I wrote the reply my parents sent back to my teacher. Dad dictated, and I put his words in writing. I had my blotter in my left hand, and my ink bottle positioned just right to prevent it from tipping over. I cleaned the nib of my pen so my writing would be clean and I had my blotter in my left hand to soaked up the ink overflow with blotter.

Dear Mr. and Mrs. Okocha,
 We are happy to receive your letter, and we will be glad to let

The Courage To Aspire

Ogbuleke travel to Umuahia with you. However, he is a young boy, and he has never visited abroad before, so we are worried about how he is going to behave in the presence of your mother and her family. Please let her know that he is growing up in the village, and he has never lived with people as enlightened and educated as you. Tell her also we are happy she picked him to visit her and her family.

Have a safe journey.

Sincerely,
Mr. and Mrs. Ikebie Ndukwe

    On Tuesday morning after the morning assembly, I got permission from the headmaster, went next door, and handed the letter to Mrs. Okocha. Then I returned to my seat. Uncle Okereke heard the news, sent for me, and gave me a little box to travel with. On the last Friday before the Easter holidays, I did not go to school with other kids. Instead, I went much later dressed in my Christmas clothes feeling proud and went straight to the headmaster's residence with my box containing English textbook, notebook, pencil and two pairs of shorts and two shirts.
    When I arrived at the headmaster's house, pieces of luggage were everywhere on the floor. School closed around noon, and within a few minutes, Mr. and Mrs. Okocha came home.
"Is everybody ready?" he asked.
"No, I will be ready in a few minutes," his wife replied.
"Mathew, put our luggage in the trunk and check oil and petrol. Lydia, sit on the left; Ikebie, get in the middle; and Mathew, sit on the right side," he ordered.
Mr. Okocha sat on the passenger's side, and Mrs. Okocha drove all the way to Umuahia. When we arrived at Mrs. Rose Okocha's compound, the car drove up to the front of a beautiful house, almost like the rest house beside my school's soccer field. An elderly woman of average stature came out smiling, spread her arms, and hugged me.
"You must be Ikebie," she said.
"Yes, ma'am, my name is Ogbuleke Ikebie."

"Come inside the house." She took my hand and led the way to the house, and at that moment, I had to pee so badly.

"Ma'am, I want to urinate," I said.

She pointed at the urinal. I managed to close the door before urine pressed hard and almost rushed out.

She practically took me away from everybody else.

"My son cannot stop talking about you, so I wanted to see who he has been talking about," she said.

She took me to the kitchen where she was cooking dinner. Her kitchen was so decorative with shining silver pans and pots hanging everywhere. When she began to slice a small yellow-looking fruit, my eyes began to burn and tear up.

"Ma'am, what's that thing?" I asked. "It's making my eyes burn."

"It's called the onion. Go back to the parlor. I will come and get you when I finish cutting it," Mama Rose said apologetically.

I joined Lydia in the parlor as she had just finished unpacking and was getting ready to take her bath.

Mama Rose came in the parlor and beckoned to me to return to the kitchen. I helped her whenever she needed help.

"I wish I could keep you here with me forever," she said.

I did not see much of Mr. and Mrs. Okocha until dinnertime, as they were in a separate section of the building. I helped put the plates, spoons, and forks on the table. Then I gave everybody their napkins before I sat down.

Somehow, I forgot I was a visitor and kept helping Mama Rose. She was a kind and sweet woman like my mom.

"Ikebie, say the grace," the headmaster said.

"Close your eyes. God is good. God is gracious. God, we thank you for getting us here safely. We thank you for the food we are about to eat. Bless it for us, and I thank you for Mama Rose. Amen." I opened my eyes.

"I can see why you keep talking about Ikebie. This boy is a sweet little thing. Can I keep him?" Mama Rose asked Mrs. Okocha.

"The time he spent Easter break with us back at the school, the only thing he did not do was cooking, and he felt happy doing it," Lydia said.

"His mother is a lucky woman," Mama Rose said

The Courage To Aspire

"Are you saying that I wasn't a sweet child when I was young?" the headmaster asked humorously.

"My dear, you were sweet," she replied.

After dinner, I cleared the table, and Lydia and I washed the dishes. Mathew did not say a lot. I had the feeling he was not thrilled with me being there and behaving the way I did, but I did not know any better. Shortly, he went back to his room, and I sat with the family while they talked about this and that uncle who they said came around, continually asking for money.

"Lydia, when are you taking Ikebie to the township?" Mama Rose asked.

"Helen and I are attending a meeting at the Uzuakoli Methodist College tomorrow," the headmaster said. "When we return, Mathew will take them around the township and the government secondary school."

While they were gone, I helped Mama Rose plant some seeds in the garden. I went to the pump with Lydia to fetch water. Their water ran out of pipes, unlike ours, which ran out of the rocky hill by the waterside. They did not have a stream where we could go and play in the water. I guess you don't need a stream when you have a pipe carrying water straight to your compound. We made two trips to the pump.

"What happened to Mathew?" I asked.

"He went to Uzuakoli with Mr. and Mrs. Okocha. He is their driver," she said.

Mr. and Mrs. Okocha returned very late in the evening after we had eaten dinner. Chatting and laughing as they walked in the house. Lydia took Mrs. Okocha's pocketbook, and I Mr. Okocha's briefcase. Lydia and I served them dinner before we went to bed.

The following day, Mathew took Lydia and me to the township. The township was smoky, smelling like coal, and trains were coming and going nonstop as people crowded the platform waiting for trains. We visited the government secondary school before going back to the village. For the most part, I played soccer with the kids in the village. On Friday, we returned home.

When we were leaving, Mama Rose hugged me, and I kept looking back at her from inside the car until she abruptly went out of sight. One extraordinary thing about the trip was how everything—houses, trees, and people—kept running back as the car drove past them.

We arrived at the headmaster's residence early in the afternoon and then I went home right away, eager to tell Mom about Mama Rose. When I got back, Mom was sleeping with Nwakego while Anyele sat all alone. We went outside to avoid waking Mom up; she did not sleep in the afternoon that often. I gave him a biscuit, and then we went to the square and stayed there until dinnertime. At dinner, I told Mom she and Mama Rose were alike.

"Maa, she called me a sweet little thing, and she wanted to keep me," I said.

"She was joking," Mom said.

"Did you enjoy yourself?" Dad asked.

"Yes, I did."

"Did you behave well?" he asked again.

"Yes, I think so," said I.

On Monday morning, school resumed. Having slept in the same house and having served the headmaster, I had mixed feelings about how to act in the classroom. I stopped jumping out of my seat to solve problems on the blackboard.

In June, we had a very unusual midyear examination. The question and answer sheets were different. Time and items allowed in the classroom were very different. When the results came out, the result sheet had one of the two comments on it: "ready" and "not ready." The students who scored "ready" went on advanced lessons, while the others continued as usual. I was one of the ready students. All the ready students, except for me, filled out secondary school entrance examination application forms. Shortly in August, they traveled to different places to take entrance exams for their secondary school of choice. I was not among them because I had nobody to pay for my secondary school education. I was just happy to be where I was with the prospect of going to live with my brother in Aba, of all places.

The Courage To Aspire

Nwakaego had been sick for a few months. It started like fever, and we did not have hospitals, so Uncle Okereke gave her pills, and a dibia treated her with herbs, but she did not get better. I would carry her and try to get her to eat something, but she could not get anything down—not even light soup. She emaciated and got weaker, but I continued to believe she would recover. Mom began to wither away like a plant on contaminated soil. Two weeks later, Nwakaego passed at midnight while I was sleeping, and Dad woke me up.

"Ogbu, Nwakaego has passed. Meet me at the backyard," he said.

For the first time, I had a strange feeling—emptiness and fear. I wanted to see Mom, but many people were surrounding her.

I met Dad at the backyard, where he was digging up a grave to bury her. I helped him as tears rolled down my eyes until we reached the right depth. Mom was screaming and rolling around on the ground.

"Why did you allow this? Why didn't you take me? She is a young soul; a child this young does not deserve to die so early. Good God, where are you? What did I do wrong?" she kept screaming.

After preparing the grave, all the elders offered their native ritual, Dad chewed odo—a yellow substance derived from a plant; nzu—a slab of chalk; and osoji—a spicy nut. Natives believe the combination has protective power against the devil. Then he spat it all over the grave. The elders lit oil lamps and placed them at the four sides of the grave.

"Ogbu, I want you to give your sister her last bath, as you used to do when she was alive. I know she would want you to do that," Dad said.

Her body was flabby and flexible. I struggled, picked her up, and carried her to the grave. I gave her a bath and wrapped her in a white cloth, and the elders lowered her into the grave. We walked down to the stream and bathed. When we returned home, the oldest dibia in the village sprinkled some liquid on us with his oxtail, and then we went back to bed.

From that day, Mom—who had been flourishing and blossoming—began to fade and wither like a flower in the winter. She cried every day and every night, forcing me to cry too.

"I want another daughter; I need a girl," she kept saying.

She began to travel everywhere to see dibias (native doctors), so they could help her to conceive another girl. She agonized until she lost the will to smile, her cheekbones began to protrude, and tears began to run down my eyes. One day we were sitting in the kitchen, then I put my hands around her neck and looked into her blurry eyes and said:

"Maa, if you stop looking for another daughter, I will do everything girls do for their mother," I said. "Stop sleeping with Dad; I don't want you to die."

She hugged me and held me tight for a while, and then she looked into my face as tears ran down her face and mine.

"OK, let's cook," she said.

I visited Egbichi and told her what I said to Mom. Then she told her mother and other girls. Every day after school, I went to the stream with the girls and filled our drinking-water pot with water, and ground condiments for Mom to cook with when she got home from the farm. I went with the girls to fetch firewood for cooking, and I cracked palm kernels for Mom. A few days later, she called me to the kitchen.

"I want you to know that you are an exceptional young man," she said. "I will do what you said. I have thought about it, and I realized that I am lucky to have you and your brothers as my children. I told your father, don't worry about me anymore."

A few weeks later, on a Saturday afternoon, the Christ Apostolic Church held an open prayer meeting at the square. They sang and danced, and their pastor preached to the crowd. After the meeting, their visiting missionary from America pointed at Mom and invited her to worship with them on Sunday. She went to church on Sunday, and from that day, she was never the same woman I used to know.

She attended Bible studies, prayer meetings, and church services. Surprisingly, she did not ask me to go to church with her. It did not take long before her spirituality began to show. One day after church, Mom told Dad to take the lock off her door.

"Why do you want to do that?" Dad asked.

"So that people can come in and eat when they are hungry," she said.

"Are you sure you are not losing your mind?" he asked.

"No, I am not losing my mind. I feel good about it; don't worry," Mom said.

The Courage To Aspire

Dad took the lock off her door, and every day, girls from my village—who had heard I was doing things for Mom that girls do for their mother—came to our house and filled our pots with water and got all the ingredients ready for Mom to cook within the evening. Some days they prepared food for her, and when she got home, she served the food. Gradually, Mom began to regain her happy demeanor. She let those girls come around when she was home, and she entertained them.

✱✱✱

Early in November, many students who had taken the secondary-school entrance examination began to receive letters of admission. Elechi Uche got admission to Uzuakoli Methodist Secondary School, Eke Okai was already a second-year student there, and others were going to other secondary schools. Their future road maps seemed clear; at least it looked that way.

One Friday morning in November, the headmaster announced that the final exam would start on the first Monday of December. "A few members of the teaching staff, including me, will be a way to conduct the exam at different schools," he said. "Be on your best behavior and good luck."

The exam started on the first Monday of December, as announced, and lasted for one week. Immediately after the exam, most of the seniors left for various reasons. My best friend, Ejere Igwe, was one of those admitted to Methodist Teacher Training College in Ovim. I was happy for him, but could not help feeling devastated at the thought of our eventual separation. However, going to live with my brother in Aba was good enough for me.

On the final day of school, the morning devotion started early. After the prayer, each teacher read out the first ten names in the class with the highest scores, not necessarily in the order of merit, followed by the names of those who had failed the exam. "If you didn't hear your name, you passed the exam, and you will be promoted when school resumes next year. Have a Merry Christmas," the headmaster said.

Chapter 9
Short Visit Abroad

It was a delightful visit;-perfect, in being much too short.

~ Jane Austen

On my last day at Alayi Methodist Central School, we went to school as pine trees whistled, and plants danced to the rhythm of a cool breeze that made its way into the town overnight. The weather was chilly and gray as fog and clouds mixed up to fend off the sun. Villagers lit burn fires all over the town, to keep them warm and prevent their skin from cracking.

Although I had had a wonderful time at school, I was subdued. A confluence of certain factors wrapped up in reality, and imminence sent me into the dungeon of emotional upheaval like a sudden car crash. The weight of the pain of my sister's death remained heavy in my mind, and the fragility of Mom's health left me fearful and paralyzed. Departing from Mr. and Mrs. Okocha and their family had made me weak and insecure. Somehow, I managed to make it safely home.

When I arrived home, I sat with Anyele on the sandy playground. He was drawing a bird on the sand, looking like he did not want to be bothered.

"Anyele, what are you doing?" I asked.

"I am drawing a bird," he replied.

"What kind of bird?"

"I don't know."

"I am going to Mama Anya's house. Do you want to go with me?"

"No, I do not want to go."

When I got to Egbichi's house, she was grinding beans for her mother.

The Courage To Aspire

"I am distraught," I said.

"About what?" she asked.

"You know that I am going to Aba on Saturday to join my brother, and I'm afraid of leaving Mom alone," I explained.

"Don't worry about her; she will be all right," she said.

When I came back home, a group of girls were entering Mom's house with buckets of drinking water.

"Everything is filled with water," Ejije said. "We will come back with firewood."

Watching those girls and realizing how sweet and kind they've been to us, tears ran down my cheeks.

"Why are you crying?" she asked.

"Nothing—seeing you act like my sister brings tears to my eyes," I said.

"We like you; we admire how much you love your mother, and we love her too," she said.

Mom had gone to pray for a sick young girl in the nearby compound and getting home as some girls—who were cooking in her kitchen tried to leave our house immediately when she entered the kitchen, she yelled.

"Where are you going?"

"We are going home," they replied.

"No, no way—we will eat together before you go home," Mom said.

"I heard that you passed standard six, young man," she said.

I ran out of the kitchen as she tried to hug me in front of those girls. When the dinner was ready, Mom asked them to eat with us, but they were too shy, so Mom served them in the kitchen. At dinner, I asked Mom and Dad if they could let me spend the weekend with my surrogate mother, Mama Ugo Okereke, and they were elated to hear my request judging from the smile on their faces.

"That is very thoughtful. I will escort you there tonight, so you can go to the farm with Mama Ugo tomorrow," Dad said.

"No, I will go in the morning; it's too late now," I replied.

"OK, I will wake you up early, so you can get to her house before they go to work," he said.

Chuks I. Ndukwe

I cannot remember sleeping that night. I only remember lying in bed and staring at the thatched roof, closing my eyes a million times, and hoping I would open them and find myself at Mama Ugo's house. However, every time I opened my eyes, I was still lying in my bed. By the time daylight began to creep into the room, I was already awake, waiting for Dad to open the door. Immediately, when I heard the screeching sound of the door, I got up and greeted Dad.

"Is it too early for me to leave?"

"No, it's just the right time; you can leave now. I will tell your mother," he said.

I left the house, half running and half walking until I got to Mama Ugo's house, as they were just opening their doors, and she was coming out of the outhouse.

"Ogbu, what's wrong?" she asked.

"Nothing is wrong. I want to spend the weekend with you. I am going to Aba on Saturday, and will not see you for a long time. I will miss you," I said.

I helped her in the kitchen to prepare rice and fried plantain for breakfast and tea to go with it. As I was taking plates to the living room, Uncle Okereke made his way to the urinal. By the time he came back to the living room, everything was on the table, and we were ready to eat.

"Ogbuleke, what is wrong?" he asked.

"I came to spend the weekend with Mama Ugo before I leave for Aba on Saturday."

The next Saturday, Mom and Egbichi escorted me to the motor park. We waited for Aba-bound lorry. It was not always obvious which lorry was going where, so when the lorry gets to the hilltop, the conductor shouts the name of their destination. We sat there and watched Uwadiegwu, Item Cooperatives, and Igbere Farmers Union vehicles stop and take off. Finally, "Ogadimma," crawled up the hill and came to a stop.

"Aba, Aba," the conductor yelled. Mom paid the fare; then we hugged, and tears rolled down our cheeks. I tried to climb up into the lorry, but Egbichi grabbed me again; she was engaged and waiting to join her husband. We hugged, and we cried. "Friend, I will miss you," she said. "Please write and let me know you made it as soon as you get

The Courage To Aspire

to Aba. Go—the lorry is taking off." Then I climbed into the lorry.

The conductor had just helped me take my seat when the clunky, old lorry rolled down the hill. It was fun riding on the lorry. We stopped at every motor park as people got out and others got in the lorry. We stopped at Isu, Akoli, Uzuakoli, and Umuahia motor parks before reaching Aba in the evening—as the sun was leaving the city and a deep-pink, lined the horizon. Ogadimma pulled into the motor park as the electric light beamed down from the poles. The park was bustling with passengers—some waiting to get on the buses, Lorries, and others, like me, arriving from different parts of Nigeria. A line of buses was leaving for Lagos, Owerri, and Onitsha—while another line of buses and Lorries were coming from those cities. The sight was surreal.

The lorry finally came to a stop after a painful maneuver directed by the park conductors. When I got off the lorry, I was in awe, wide-eyed and unable to blink. People walked around aimlessly in search of the right vehicle to take them to their destination. The signs in the park intended to help passengers locate the right vehicle were of no use. Finally, the conductor unloaded the lorry, and I was able to identify my baggage. I tried different ways to get my box and bag on top of my head, with no success; then a middle-aged man, who seemed to be waiting for the arrival of his relative, helped me lift my box with the bag on it and placed it on my head.

"Do you know where you are going?" the man asked.

"No, but somebody is around somewhere in the park waiting for me," I replied.

"Is this your first time coming to Aba?" he asked.

"Yes, this is my very first time," I replied.

"Do you know the address of the place you are going to?"

"Yes, twenty-one Danfodio Road," I answered, showing him the piece of paper on which I had written the address.

"That is very good. Look, if you can't find the person who is waiting for you, call 'taxi!' and give the driver the address; he will take you to the house," he instructed.

After getting help from that stranger, I made my way to the main road confronted with the challenge of getting my baggage down from my head without dropping everything. I do not know if there would

Chuks I. Ndukwe

have been a better or a more sophisticated technique for accomplishing this, but I came up with one that a young mind like mine could conceive. I went down on one knee and bent forward until the bag slid down to the ground gently. Then I put my box beside it and sat down. Across the street, a group of young girls under the electric pole was standing by their tables full of all kinds of food items and snacks—not unlike the group of girls who came to my school to sell identical items.

The constant buzzing up and down the road by vehicles of all makes and models captivated me. Suddenly, a dark young man of average height with broad shoulders stopped by my side and stretched out his hand to help me get up.

"Ogbuleke," he called out.

"Yes," I answered.

"My name is Elendu. I am your brother," he said.

That did not sound right. I knew I had only one older brother, Dick, and Mom and Dad never talked about any other brother. I got up with this strange man's help, and as I was staring at him and just about to ask him what he meant by "brother," he hailed a taxi, and the taxi turned around and stopped at the spot I was sitting.

"Please take us to twenty-one Danfodio Road. Ogbuleke, get in the car," he ordered. He put my baggage in the trunk. Then we drove along one road and turned into another, crossing many streets. The sight of kids and people of all ages walking around brought calm to my bewildered mind. We passed a few bridges. As we drove over one bridge, I saw a field with cows roaming around, unsure of how much longer they would live. Then I saw one of the cows dragged down by ropes tied around its horns and legs—an awful reminder that its time had come, and its destination was the slaughter pit. A short distance from that field, we passed another bridge and turned left and right, and then we were at our house.

Elendu paid the taxi driver before we got out of the car, and then he opened the trunk and gave us my baggage. Inside the house, my brother Dick, Uncle Udensi, and his wife were sitting on the couch listening to the radio as the commentator was screaming out names of soccer players who were controlling the ball in a game played somewhere—they'd never seen. I greeted them, expecting a warm response, but they

The Courage To Aspire

ignored me. I was not sure whether they did not notice us or deliberately indifferent.

"Change your clothes, and take a bath," Elendu said and pointed to the bathroom.

"Why did they ignore us like that?" I asked.

"Don't worry. When the adults are listening to a soccer game, you don't disturb them—I mean ever," he said.

"How can they listen to the game when they can't see the players?"

"Radio brings the commentary over the air," he explained.

I did not understand anything he said. I did not know if he was trying to confuse me by using big words like "radio" and "commentary."

"Let's go to the kitchen," he said.

We got to the kitchen where he cooked, and I helped with whatever he wanted me to do. When he finished cooking, we ate in the kitchen. Then we waited for the game to be over before serving our relatives inside the living room.

While we were eating, Elendu began to ask me questions.

"How are Auntie Nwaka and Father Ikebie?"

"They are fine," I answered.

"Did you see Father Kanu before leaving?"

"No, I didn't. I did not have time to go over there to see father, Kanu."

"We heard about the death of your sister, and we were devastated—especially your brother Dick," he said.

He was asking me questions as if he was my brother for real. "Who is this man?" I wondered, wishing Mom were around to explain things to me. Then the game ended, and Jenny came out first.

"Hello, Ogbuleke, welcome. Elendu, did you give Ogbuleke food yet?" she asked.

"Yes, we've eaten our dinner," Elendu answered.

I went into the house and gave my brother his letter. Surprisingly, he did not seem as excited as I was.

"Is everybody OK at home?" he asked.

"Yes, they are fine," I replied.

"What happened to Nwakego? Was she sick?" he asked.

Chuks I. Ndukwe

"Yes, she was sick for a while. Mom and Dad did everything they could," I said.

"It must have been awful to see her die like that," he said.

"Yes, I gave her the last bath and wrapped her up in a white sheet…I sobbed; then they lowered her in the grave," I said.

On Sunday, Uncle Udensi and Brother Dick went to church, but Elendu and I walked around the fun places in the township: Movie Theater, soccer stadium, and the waterside.

The following morning, we filled all the containers in the house with drinking water, and then we did what would be our weekend chores: dusting, sweeping, and mopping the floors. Then we prepared lunch. Later in the afternoon, we went swimming at the waterside.

Young people were everywhere in the water, swimming and splashing water on everybody. We joined in as I followed Elendu into the center of the river, floating like a fish.

"Oh, you think you can swim. Come on; let's go farther," Elendu challenged.

"No, I can't go farther; this river is too deep for me."

We stayed at the waterside for the whole afternoon, drying up and then going back into the water repeatedly. Finally, we washed the clothes we had with us and went home. In the evening, Elendu and I cooked dinner and I was surprised that Uncle Udensi's wife did not come to the kitchen even once.

"What does Jenny do?" I asked.

"She stays in the bedroom. She does not even like to sit in the living room to chat with anybody. I don't know what she does; maybe you can find out," Elendu snapped.

On Sunday, we went to Ogboh hill walking along Asa Road all the way, stopping briefly at some places like the Cinema Theater to check out what movie was showing. When we got to Ogboh hill, the waterside was better than the previous site. There were places to lie down and relax and restaurants in which to sit and eat, and girls were all over the place selling different things.

The most enjoyable part of the location was the bridge. Kids were jumping and diving into the water from the deck. I walked around for a while, trying to familiarize myself with the waterside. I watched kids

The Courage To Aspire

jump and dive from both sides of the bridge. Finally, I took off my clothes and joined the action. At first, I was scared.

The bridge was very high, and I had not jumped from a deck that high before. As I was trying to summon enough courage, Elendu pushed me, and I was in the water swimming without complaining. I got out of the water and dived from the opposite side of the bridge.

After a while, a neighbor, Eze, joined me. We lay down and chatted about school and his brother's business, my brother's business, and how much fun he was having in high school—college as they called it.

"Look over there; that's Elendu with some girl," he said.

"Yes, I know. We came together; then Elendu saw that girl and left me," I said.

"Are you ready to go?" he asked.

"Yes," I replied.

We told Elendu we were leaving.

"Wait, I'm coming with you," he said.

On the following Sunday, Elendu and I went to "Over-rail" to watch the Europeans play golf. I'd never seen golf before, so the game seemed a little strange. People kept hitting the ball and walked a long distance to hit it again. It was boring for me, so I played soccer while Elendu watched. The range was a long one, and later in the evening, my legs got sore. Elendu gave me some jelly to rub on them, and then we went to the pump to fetch water. After dinner, I could not do anything or go anywhere. I lay in the backyard until it was time to go to bed.

"Where did you go today?" Eze asked.

"I went out with Elendu to the European quarters to watch them play golf," I answered.

"That's a long walk," he said.

"That's why my legs are sore."

"You should stop following Elendu around," he cautioned.

"Why?"

"He has a bad reputation."

On Monday, I told Elendu about people and places I'd like to visit.

"I want to visit Uncle Emeke Chima," I said.

"We can do that on Sunday," he replied. "Do you know that Dick used to be his houseboy?"

Chuks I. Ndukwe

"What is a houseboy?" I asked.

"Like we are to our brothers," he said.

"Do you mean like servants?"

"That is exactly right."

On Friday, Elendu and I went to the pump to fetch water. When we got there, he told me he had somewhere to go, so I went home by myself and made two more trips with Ukpabi, a neighbor's brother and another two trips with Eze. By that time, I had filled all the containers in our house with water.

Then Eze and I lay on a mat just by the spot where my brother and Uncle Udensi were lying on their mats chatting. Eze talked about his college, accounting and typing lessons, and the girls in his class. While we lay there chatting, Elendu came home carrying his drum of water. Jenny, Uncle Udensi's wife, said, "Every night, Elendu makes four to five trips to the pump while Ogbuleke sits with college students and chats with them about college."

My brother Dick took me into the house and slapped stars out of my eyes without asking me any questions. I was confused at first; then I collected myself and went back outside, surprised by my brother's action. They resumed their angry discussion about my behavior. Other people who had seen me making numerous trips were surprised too. The landlord wanted to protest on my behalf because he had seen me and his brother going and coming home from the pump. He had also seen me going and coming back from the pump twice with Eze, so he was infuriated. I begged him not to. As I sat down, I heard Uncle Udensi talking about how I acted superior toward Elendu.

"We will see who is going to pay for that college he's talking about," he said.

That statement pierced my heart like a dagger. I decided if he offered to pay for my college education, I would refuse it. As for my brother, I was not mad at him. I recognized he was living with Uncle Udensi out of charity. I did not believe he would hurt me intentionally.

On Sunday, I visited Uncle Emeke Chima.

"I heard that you finished standard six and you are spending your holidays here in town, and I've been trying to get hold of you," he said. "I am a member of the education committee of Bende Divisional

The Courage To Aspire

Council. We are recruiting teachers to teach in the new universal education system. I want you to go to Ozuitem on the date shown on this piece of paper. We are interviewing candidates on that day, and I will be there."

It was a significant relief, as I wanted to get away from Uncle Udensi's wife. So when I returned home, I informed them I was leaving on Friday.

"Why are you leaving? Didn't you come here to live with me?" Brother Dick asked.

I did not say a word. Surprisingly, from Monday to Thursday, they were kind to me, but I had made up my mind even though the outcome was uncertain. On Wednesday, I received a letter from Mr. Madubike Okocha asking me to come home and see him. I was glad to hear from him, especially after the deplorable way I was being treated.

Chapter 10
Encouragement and Aspiration

Just as courage has no meaning without fear, faith has no meaning without doubt. They're the yin and yang of all aspiration.

~ Dennis Palumbo

On Friday morning, while I was preparing to return home, a Peugeot 404 station wagon drove up in front of our house, and Uncle Anyele Aka rushed out of the car and into the house and asked, "Where is Ogbuleke?" he asked.

"I am right here."

"Are you ready?" he asked.

"Yes, Uncle, I am ready."

"OK, get in the car," Uncle Anyele said.

Waving and smiling at everybody, I got in the car and had a beautiful ride home with only one stop at Umuahia Motor Park to fill up the tank with petrol. At about noon, I was back home with Mom and Anyele.

"Take off those clothes and take a bath. I will prepare food for you," Mom said.

She fried plantain and served it with rice and stew. I told her what Uncle Emeke Chima had said about going to Ozuitem for an interview.

"I know about it. Nobody wants you to go into trading," she said.

"What do they want me to do? I don't have any chance of going to secondary school like kids with rich relatives."

I also told her what Uncle Udensi said—that he would not pay for my education—but I did not say anything about the nasty slap my brother had given me or anything about Uncle Udensi's wife.

"He should never have said that," Mom said. "Anyway, that statement is a challenge to God. You shouldn't worry about it."

Then I told her about Mr. Madubike Okocha's letter.

"He came here looking for you. You can go and see him on

The Courage To Aspire

Monday," she said.

On Monday, I went to Mr. Okocha's residence and knocked on the door. He opened the door with his eyeglasses hanging on his nose. He looked at me from the top of the glasses, bending his head slightly down —a typical image of him I would never forget.

"Come in, Ikebie. Do, sit down," he said.

Mrs. Okocha came out, and I stood up quickly and greeted her.

"When did you come home?" she asked. "I came home on Saturday."

"Ikebie, I filled out an application form for the entrance examination for Government Trade Center Enugu on your behalf," he said. "There is only one of its kind in the whole region, and I believe you have the best chance of getting into that school. They admit only the brightest students."

"I don't know anybody in Enugu, and I don't think Dad can afford to pay for me to go to Enugu," I said, crying.

"Why are you crying?" he asked as Mrs. Okocha looked on.

"I know you want me to become somebody and successful," I said. "But I'm afraid I can't make you proud of me, I am sorry."

"If you are invited for the exam, which consists of written and oral questions, I will pay for your trip to and from Enugu," he said. "I will also give you pocket money. The school will provide you with accommodations, so don't cry."

I jumped up and covered my face. I was in a state of disbelief.

"I don't know what to say, sir—ma'am. Please help me. I do not know what to do. Thank you, sir. I am so happy," I rattled.

"You don't need any help. You are amazing, child," Mrs. Okocha said. "Are you hungry? We have food leftover from lunch."

"No, ma'am, I'm not hungry."

"Don't leave home; I will send for you when I get the invitation," he advised.

"All right, sir. Thank you," I said and left.

I cannot remember exactly how I got home. My best guess is that I ran all the way, and judging from my past behavior under a similar euphoric state of mind, I was probably hopping and jumping from one side of the road to the other and perhaps kicking a few plants that dared stick their branches out. I could not believe Mrs. Okocha had said I was a fantastic child. Those words stuck in my mind and stayed there as indelible as words carved in stone.

Later in the afternoon, Mom came home with Anyele running behind her.

"Let me cook food for you and your brother. Then you can tell me why Okocha wanted to see you," she said.

Mom believed in discussing certain matters while eating, a theory I've never been able to substantiate. While Anyele and I munched on beans and plantain, she sat directly opposite me, then I stopped eating and look back at her.

"Now, why did that man ask you to come home?" she asked.

I told her exactly what had happened when I got to the headmaster's residence.

"First of all, I want to thank God for that man," she said. "Do you remember Miss Okorie, Mr. Okpee, and all of your teachers? Every one of them visited this house, and each one of them took you home to meet their family. Ogbu, I have nothing to say. Sure, I gave birth to you, but you are everybody's son."

When Dad came home, Mom relayed the story to him. At dinner, he looked at me and said a few words: "Ogbu, did everything go well between you and headmaster Okocha?"

"Yes, he told me to stay home."

However, I did not stay home; I thought it was a good idea to see if I could qualify to work as a teacher.

On the day of my interview for the teaching position, I traveled with a group of other young people to Bende Divisional Education Office in Ozuitem. Some of the candidates had finished standard six a few years before me. We walked a very long distance—about fifteen miles—traversing farmlands and crossing deep and wide streams (or rivers, as the natives called them). You could paddle a boat on some of them.

I was twelve, and younger than most candidates, but, after the interview, I was selected to attend the teacher-training course. The educational system was a free, universal system, and we were the first group of teachers in the system. The training started on Monday and

The Courage To Aspire

lasted for four weeks, ending with material preparation and a teaching demonstration. On the last day of training, the divisional education officer, Mr. C. U. Okereke addressed the trainees before we dispersed and returned home to wait for teaching assignments. For reasons unknown, I cannot remember how much I was paid nor what I did with the money I earned.

The Sunday after I returned home, Mr. Okocha attended church at Amankalu Methodist Church. After the service, he stopped by my house with Uncle Okereke Chima, and Azik Ukachukwu and Dad treated them to his special palm wine and Mom's Sunday delight. After the meal, we walked to the square, and before Mr. Okocha entered his car, he gave me a letter—an invitation to the GTC entrance exam.

"I want you to come to my residence on Friday before the exam day with your traveling box," he said. "Mathew will take you to the Ovim train station, where you will board the train to Enugu. I will tell you all about your trip when you come on that Friday."

On the Friday before the exam, I reported at Mr. Okocha's residence. After dinner, he called Mathew and me together.

"Tomorrow morning, Mathew will take you to Ovim train station," he said. "He will purchase a ticket for you. Keep it secure because the conductor will ask for it inside the train on your way to Enugu. When you arrive at Enugu train station, take a taxi to GTC and report to the security office at the principal's office. After the exam on Wednesday, you will go to Enugu train station and buy a ticket for Ovim. Try and get to the station early, and check the train's scheduled arrival time at Enugu, so you don't miss your train. Mathew will be at Ovim train station to bring you home." Then he gave me an envelope with money inside.

On Saturday morning, Mathew took me to Ovim train station, he bought the ticket, handed it to me, and I put it in my pocket. I observed him so I would not have any difficulty purchasing a ticket on my way back. We checked the train's arrival time and then waited until we heard a loud sound and saw smoke rising from a distance—I had seen that once before.

"Get your box; that's your train coming," Mathew said.

The train rolled into the station and came to a stop. I boarded the train and waved at Mathew as the train began to move away from the station.

The journey was simply incredible. Many government officials were in that train, and it stopped at many stations to drop off and pick up passengers on the way.

When I arrived at Enugu train station late in the evening, I hailed a taxi.

"Can you take me to GTC?" I asked the driver.

"What is going on in that college?" he asked. "I've taken so many young people there this evening."

"The college is hosting us for their entrance examination," I said.

He drove to the school campus, and the gatekeeper opened the gate after asking the driver a few questions.

I reported to the security office for processing. After verifying the information on my invitation letter, a man escorted me to a dormitory holding fifteen candidates, bringing the total number of candidates in the dormitory to sixteen. There were dormitories everywhere on the campus, and sixteen candidates occupied each one. The auditorium held more candidates than the dormitories. Candidates were boys who had come from all cities and towns in the Eastern Region of Nigeria—all vying for two hundred positions for the final interview. One of the candidates, who had been occupying the dormitory before my arrival, showed me around.

I changed my clothes, took my bath, and joined other candidates who had arrived by train in the dining hall, where the school treated us to a delicious meal.

On Monday, the day of the examination, the campus maintenance people converted the dining hall to a large classroom after breakfast. At about nine o'clock, the principal and ten other white men guided the candidates to their seats and gave instructions about the rules as well as the structure of the examination. The examination comprised of written, oral, and practical tests. Shortly after going over the instructions, they passed out the question papers, and we had one hour to complete the answers followed by oral questions and answers. Some of the questions were about current events, and some were to tell a story about a celebration or other activities.

The Courage To Aspire

On Tuesday, the process continued with practical tests with ten stations where they had pieces of wood and other materials and pictures of finished, or assembled, objects on the table. We had one minute to replicate an object from those pieces of wood and other materials. Out of the five objects we were required to reproduce, I can't remember if I finished any one of them entirely before time ran out, and I heard a mean-looking man say in an icy and calculated voice, "Time is up; you can go. Next."

I left the room with tears running down my face; it was apparent I had not done well at all.

Surprisingly, when I joined the other candidates who had gone through the exercise, everybody was sobbing and wiping away their tears.

"I'm in good company," I thought.

"How many did you complete?" a few kids asked me.

"I don't think I completed any of them right," I answered.

"Yeah, me too," other people echoed.

We stayed separated until the last candidate came out of the room. The principal who seemed to lack sympathy came out and stood in front of the sobbing candidates.

"This is the end of the day's exercise. You will be informed in a letter if you have been chosen to come back for the final examination," he announced. "Good luck and a safe journey."

We returned to our respective dormitories.

"I don't think anybody did well in that practical test," one person said.

"Let's go and play soccer in the field," another person said.

Nobody was in the mood for any kind of fun, so nobody obliged. Within one hour, workers restored the dining hall to its original formation. The campus manager rang the bell in front of the dining hall, and we went into the hall and ate our dinner. I worried about what I would tell Mr. and Mrs. Okocha when I returned home.

On Wednesday morning, I followed other candidates and bought my ticket at the train station.

Inside the train, I was pretty much detached from and oblivious to what was going on inside and outside the train. The ride did not feel as enjoyable as it did on my way to Enugu. The train arrived at Ovim train station at 2:30 p.m., and Mathew was on the platform waiting for me. I disembarked the train subdued and immobile.

"Ikebie, what is wrong?" he asked.

"Everything is wrong. I wish I did not go for that exam."

"What happened?" he asked.

"I failed the exam."

"You don't know that. You always feel pitiful after exams," Mathew said.

"Yes, but this is different."

We walked to the parking lot and got into the car; he started the engine. Then we sat there for a few minutes before we took off.

"Make sure you don't look like that when we get home," he said.

"Don't worry. I will be dead by the time we get home," I replied.

He stopped at Isukwuato Motor Park. "Come on, they have hot and steaming maimai in this park. Get some," he said.

"I don't want any," I said.

"You're right; you will be dead by the time we get home. Lydia is not home to offer you any food, so get some of this," he insisted.

"I said, no! Leave me alone," I snapped.

Now we arrived at the headmaster's residence, and he was on the verandah, reading a newspaper.

"Good afternoon, sir," I greeted him.

"Ikebie, how did it go?" he asked.

"Terrible, I am not sure I did well," I said.

Then Mrs. Okocha joined us on the verandah and took her seat by her husband.

"What made it terrible?" he asked.

"I don't think I did well."

"Tell us about the whole process," Mrs. Okocha demanded.

"We did both written and oral examination on Monday," I said.

"Did you answer all the questions on the written part?" she asked.

"Yes, ma'am," I said

"Did you have enough time to go over your answers?" she asked.

"Yes, ma'am, I did."

"In the oral part, how many questions did they ask you?"

The Courage To Aspire

"They asked us about ten questions."
"Did you answer all the questions?"
"I did, ma'am."
"Give me one example of the questions they asked."
"The interviewer wanted to know my two most favorite subjects."
"What did you say?" she asked.
"I told him Mathematics and physics are my favorites."
"What other questions did he ask?" She asked.
"He asked me what I thought would happen if I kicked a ball at the wall and why."
"And?" the headmaster asked.
"I told him that the ball will bounce back with the equivalent force I kicked it because for every action, there is an equal and opposite reaction."
"Go on to the practical part of the tests," she said.
"On Tuesday we did practical tests. They gave me pieces of wood and other materials to construct an object in a picture. I had only one minute to replicate each of the five objects on the picture."
"Like a blueprint," Mr. Okocha said, looking at his wife.
"How many did you finish?"
"I don't think I finished any of them," I said.
"How about the other candidates?" she asked.
"Everybody sobbed after the tests."
"Don't worry anymore," she said.
"I think you did well," Mr. Okocha added. "Go home and get some rest."

A few weeks later, Uncle Okereke Chima went to court; he was the secretary of the local council, so he helped the court clerk to decide cases. On his way home, Mr. Okocha gave him an official envelope to give to me and asked him to tell me to see him right away. The envelope was not sealed, and I knew what it was all about.

"Congratulations, you have been selected to attend the final examination on the date specified. I look forward to seeing you again," the letter read.

On the following day, I went straight to Mr. Okocha's residence. The front door was open, and Mathew was standing in the backyard. I raised the letter and waved it at him. "Where is the headmaster?" I asked

"He will be right back. He and Mrs. Okocha take a walk to the courtyard and back every day after school," he said.

"I know that," I said, just to remind him I wasn't a stranger in the house. We kicked a ball back and forth in the backyard until Mr. and Mrs. Okocha came back through the gate at the backyard.

"Ikebie, you got my message," the headmaster said.

"Yes, I did, sir," I replied.

"Congratulations," he said.

"Thank you, sir," I said.

"Come here on Friday before the final exam; we will repeat what we did the first time."

"I will, sir," I said and left.

On the Friday before the exam, I went to Mr. Okocha's residence and spent the night. On Saturday, he gave me enough money for the round trip, and Mathew took me to the train station, where I boarded the train to Enugu.

On Monday, there were much fewer candidates than before, and we had a written exam in English language, mathematics, and physics.

The exam lasted for four hours with a few minutes break in between. I spent a day at the school campus. The school had a lovely soccer field, so we played soccer on Tuesday evening. On Wednesday, I boarded the train, and Mathew was waiting for me at Ovim train station. I did not feel as bad as I did after the first exam when I disembarked the train.

"You look happy," Mathew commented.

"I don't feel bad," I said.

When we arrived home, Mr. and Mrs. Okocha were walking back from the courthouse. So we stopped and picked them up.

"Good afternoon, ma'am," I said.

"Ikebie, how did you do?" Mrs. Okocha asked.

"I don't think I did badly this time."

"Did you answer all the questions for each paper?" she asked.

"Yes, ma'am, and I reviewed my answers three times on each occasion."

"You know that if we get a letter from the school, you are in," Mr.

The Courage To Aspire

Okocha said.

"I am aware of that, sir."

***

Nigeria had just gained independence, and the federal government established a free, universal education system. (Primary education was not free of charge until then hence divisional education authorities were recruiting candidates with a minimum qualification of standard six to teach in the new system). I had received my assignment to teach at Okpufu Universal Primary School—under Mr. Okorie Gbaningo.

When school started, we registered 144 pupils—boys and girls. All free, universal primary schools in the nation began from elementary one; therefore, every teacher taught elementary one.

I waited for a long time without getting any mail from GTC. I consoled myself with the thought that I was a teacher and could start making plans for the future—like going to the teacher-training college...or secondary high school, for that matter, if I saved enough money. All sorts of thoughts came to mind, and one thing was clear: I was not going to be a jewelry trader like my brother. I enjoyed teaching; I remembered my first year in elementary school and how Miss Okorie took care of me, so I treated my pupils the same.

One Friday evening, I was returning from Ozuitem Divisional Education Office—teachers went there to get their pay every month, and I had stopped by Uncle Okereke's house with the intention of spending the night but Mama Ugo told me that Uncle Okereke had gone to our house to give me a letter from Mr. Okocha.

I jumped up. "Maa, I will see you tomorrow at the church," I said and took off running.

I was flying like a bird; the pain I had been feeling in my legs dissipated immediately. I met Uncle Okereke on his way back home.

"I stopped by your house to spend the night, and Mama Ugo told me that you went to give me a letter from Mr. Okocha," I said.

"That is correct. The letter is from the Ministry of Education in Enugu," he said.

"Thank you. I will see you at the church tomorrow," I said and took off running again.

I got home, and Dad gave me the envelope which I ripped open immediately.

"Congratulations," the letter said. "You have been selected to attend this historic institution beginning on the above date. The school is free of charge and provides students with pocket money every week. Plan to arrive at the school campus no later than two days before the beginning of the school term."

Tears of joy rolled down my eyes; nobody from my town had ever gained admission to GTC before. When my excitement subsided, I told Mom and Dad. "I want you to go to the central school and see your headmaster; let's make sure the letter is real," Dad said. Probably he had a good reason to be skeptical.

On Sunday, after church service, I went to see Mr. and Mrs. Okocha. When I got there, they were relaxing and listening to the radio then I knocked on the door.

"Come in," Mrs. Okocha said.

"Good afternoon, ma'am."

"You got the good news," Mr. Okocha said.

"Yes, sir, I did. I don't know how to thank you and Mrs. Okocha," I said.

"Ikebie, sit down," he said. "Do you remember the day we had a visitor from America, and he performed a demonstration in the classroom, and you jumped up excited? And every time I asked the class to write, an essay on what you wanted to be when you grew up—every single time—you wrote about being an electrical engineer? I am proud to be your teacher, and Mrs. Okocha is even more pleased. You can thank us by being the kind of student at GTC that you were here in your primary school and going on to become an electrical engineer.

"Lydia cooked some rice; go to the kitchen and get some. I hope to see you before you leave for GTC. Congratulations again," he concluded.

I began to cry; I could not hold it in as tears flowed down my cheeks like water.

When I got home, Mom was finishing dinner, so I went into the kitchen to help her.

The Courage To Aspire

"Go—you are a teacher now; you don't have to set up the plates anymore," she said.

Mom and I cried when I told her and Dad what Mr. Okocha had said.

"How can such a good deed make you cry like that?" Dad asked. "You should be happy and thankful to God."

From that day until the end of the school year, I was relaxed. I went to school every day, happy and hopeful. I did my best to encourage the kids to enjoy coming to school and to learn with enthusiasm. At the end of the school year, I resigned from my teaching position. And before I left home for GTC, I spent a week with Uncle Okereke and Mama Ugo, and two days at Mr. and Mrs. Okocha's residence with their family.

Chapter 11
Spiritual Enrichment

All knowledge pursued merely for the enrichment of personal learning and the accumulation of personal treasure leads you away from the path; but all knowledge pursued for growth to ripeness within the process of human ennoblement and cosmic development brings you a step forward.

~ Rudolf Steiner

School has just ended, and the motor parks crowded with students who had come to get on those clunky lorries to take them to places they would spend Christmas holidays with their relatives. The weather had transformed my town into an exotic paradise where birds chirped loudly and flew low unafraid, gray fog covered the town, and lovers walked close to each other but never held hands—afraid natives would stare at them. Bluish clouds hung low, preventing the sun above it from piercing through to burn the fog. Burn fires glowed in every compound, in every village, and natives folded their hands across their chests. I cannot remember if that was enough to warm the body. Nevertheless, it was a small but joyful part of the year.

"My father, Ndukwe, would have been proud to see you today," Dad said.

From dinner until bedtime, Mom sat near me—not by the side, but directly opposite squeezing my hands, looked squarely in my eyes and talked about God, Jesus Christ, and the essence of life and simple living—rooted firmly in humility and cleanliness of body and spirit. I would look back in her face with an unflinching stare. No doubt, Mom was in her most comfortable domain. She has always been there and emphasized the same sermon—virtues of decent living but that time she drilled it more in-depth than ever. Finally, she took my hand—stretched

The Courage To Aspire

it and began.

"Ogbu, promise me that you will keep this palm of yours as clean as it is today till you return to your creator," she demanded.

First, my palm was not clean because I had been playing outside, second, how could I accomplish or keep such a promise? I wondered. I stared at her, amazed she could ask me to promise what I considered impractical if not totally impossible.

"I know you will. Remain humble and keep that palm clean. If you do, there is no obstacle too high or pain so severe you cannot overcome. Get some sleep," she said, pressing my head on her chest.

When my head was resting on Mom's chest, I experienced a sudden jolt and momentary loss of presence. Two thoughts came to mind: First, I was lying on the chest, which fed and calmed me—her baby when I was distressed. Second, I had asked her to stop looking for a daughter for fear of losing her, she did, and she had found spirituality and happiness in the word of God and company of my village's girls. That moment was transformational—a double transfusion of spirituality that stuck deep in my heart. Then she finished by saying this:

"Every uncommon event happens for a reason when it is not obvious, you must search for it; sometimes it is in the hand of the person next to you."

I lay in bed awake all night thinking about the jolt and cool chill-like-current that had flowed through my body when my head was resting on Mom's chest. In the morning, I ate breakfast and punched Anyele around just to watch him giggle again. I got a warm embrace from Dad.

"Be careful," he advised.

Then Mom escorted me to the motor park. Just as she was putting my box down, a Peugeot 404 station wagon flew up the hill and stopped. Uncle Anyaele, the driver, came out and hugged Mom.

"Ogbuleke, are you returning to Aba?" he asked.

"Yes, Uncle, I am."

"Get in front," he ordered.

I got in the car and waved at Mom, and the vehicle took off, flying. We passed many motor parks and made short stops at a few to pick up passengers who were traveling without company and with light luggage.

"I've already made my money for the day; we can ride empty," he said. He drove straight to forty-six Ulasi Road and let me off.

"Don't worry about the fare," he said.

It was about two o'clock in the afternoon. Uncle Emeke's wife, Auntie Ugo, took my box.

"I've got to go to the store to greet my uncles first," I said.

Standing at the end of the hallway is a little girl—about four years old. I walked past her and went to the backyard to greet my other uncles' wives, and told them I was going to the store to greet my uncles. That little girl screamed.

"Uncle, I am coming with you."

"Do you know where I am going?" I asked.

"To the store," she answered.

On our way to the store, she kept hopping up and down, up and down, holding my hand so tightly she almost pulled me down.

Occasionally, I looked down, and she looked happy and spirited. We got to the store, packed with customers pushing each other to get to the textiles they liked, but I managed to greet Uncle Okorie Onwuchekwa. Before we left, he gave us money to buy roasted groundnut. I bought salted, ash-roasted peanut and gave it to that little girl. She gave it back to me, and then I took some and gave her the rest. We munched on our treat as we walked home. It had not been long since I lost my sister, who had filled every moment I spent with her with happiness and joy, and I was still grieving. Unexpectedly, that little girl broke into my heart and occupied the vacuum left by my sister. We got home, then she went inside Uncle Okrie's room, came out with a towel, took my hand, and led me to the bathroom.

"Come and take your bath," she said.

I went to the bathroom and took a long bath, thinking how wonderful it was for that little girl to lift up my spirit the way she did on my arrival. I remembered Mom's words: "every uncommon event happens for a reason."

Coming out of the bathroom, I asked auntie Ugo who that girl really was.

"Auntie, what is the name of that little girl?"

The Courage To Aspire

"Oh, that's Tereza's daughter," she said. "Grace, come here. This is your uncle, Ogbuleke."

I hugged her, and she ran right back to the backyard. After dinner, I told Uncle Emeke I had resigned from teaching.

I think he almost lost his mind, horrified, and without letting me finish, he yelled. "Do you know how secure your position was in that system?"

"I was admitted to GTC Enugu," I said.

"What did you say?" he asked.

"I am leaving for GTC in two weeks," I said.

He sat down subdued and stared at me with an air of abject amazement and disbelief. "How did that happen?" he asked.

"My headmaster and his wife, Mr. and Mrs. Okocha, did everything," I answered.

"What everything did they do?" Uncle Emeke asked.

"He filled out the entrance examination application form on my behalf, he paid for my train ticket on two occasions, and his driver took me to and from Ovim train station on those two occasions to travel to Enugu to take the entrance examination."

"Are you talking about the headmaster of the Methodist Central School?" he asked.

"Yes sir, I am," I answered.

"Amazing," he said.

The next Sunday, I visited my brother Dick and Uncle Udensi at 21 Danfodio Road to let them know I was admitted to GTC Enugu and will travel to Enugu the following Friday.

"Are you talking about Government Technical College, Enugu?" Uncle Udensi asked.

"Yes."

"That's fantastic," Uncle Udensi said.

On Friday, Uncle Anyaele, the driver took me to the train station, from where I boarded the train to Enugu. When I arrived at the school, the principal's office and the security office were open, but the campus manager's office was closed. I reported to the principal's office with my admission letter, and his secretary told me I made a severe mistake. The letter stated that prospective students should arrive at the school for two days, not two weeks, before the beginning of the school term.

It was too late for me to go back home, so the security officers opened one dormitory for me, but beds had not been set up, so I slept on the bare cement floor. After a week, I began to cough, and by the time the campus manager's office and the medical center opened, I was coughing up blood.

The school nurse led me to Enugu General Hospital. After hours of tests and X-rays, the doctor said that I had tuberculosis and sent me to the infirmary unit of the hospital. The school nurse visited every day, and the cooking staff brought food three times a day. Two beautiful nurses, Iyabo and Abisola, cared for me. They asked for my textbooks and taught me basic algebra and English language while I was in the hospital. One evening, five weeks after my admission, I was playing in the field and had stopped coughing up sputum.

"You have visitors; they are coming from the main hospital," the nurse said. "The doctor has just notified us."

A few minutes later, I saw two men walking down the hill to the infirmary.

"Here they come," Iyabo said.

"They are my uncles," I said.

I ran inside the ward and put my mask on. Then I came back outside to meet them as they were chatting with Iyabo, and I could hear her say, "He's got pulmonary pneumonia, not tuberculosis."

"How long is he going to stay in the hospital?" Uncle Okorie asked.

"He's not coughing out any sputum, so I would say as soon as we get his X-ray back and his lungs have healed sufficiently well," she said.

"Ogbuleke, do you need any money?" Uncle Okereke asked.

"No, I don't need any money, the school cooking staff brings me food here," I replied.

"Nurse, how bad is the damage to his lungs?" Uncle Okorie asked.

"Not seriously—only one rib is affected, but it will heal."

"OK, Ogbuleke write to us when you go back to school. Bye, nurse, bye Ogbuleke," they greeted.

They climbed the hill until I could not see them anymore. It was

The Courage To Aspire

unbelievable that they had come all the way to Enugu General Hospital Infirmary unit to see me. I hoped they would not let Mom know. As for Dad, he would not let Mom hear something as worrisome as that; he was very protective of her. I wanted to go back to school so I could write to everybody and let them know I was well.

One week later, the result of my X-ray came back and I was well enough to go back to school but had to report to the outpatient ward two days a week for three months.

Before I left the hospital, I arranged with the nursing staff to treat me whenever I arrived at the hospital, so I could get treatment and get back to school before the beginning of classes. The principal granted me permission to leave the school campus as early as I could on Mondays and Wednesdays until the doctor certified I was well enough to stop treatment. I gave the campus manager a copy of the permission slip, and I carried a copy with me in case the security official caught me leaving through one of the open cracks on the fence—behind the campus. On the days of my treatment, I left the school as early as five o'clock in the morning and walked along the railroad tracks to the hospital.

I received treatment as soon as I arrived at the ward, and then I returned to school by the school bus that brought students to the hospital every day. Throughout my treatment as an outpatient, I did not miss any class. One morning, somebody saw me leaving the campus at five o'clock and reported to the principal. I did return to school before breakfast, as usual, and I was in class when the principal sent for me.

"Aren't you supposed to attend outpatient treatment this morning?" he asked.

"Yes, sir. I did this morning, and I am back already," I answered.

"I have a complaint that you snuck out of the campus," he said.

"Yes, sir, I did. I left at five o'clock so I could be treated and come back to school on the school bus before breakfast." I gave him the permission slip he had signed.

"Oh, yes, that's right," he said and sent me back to the class.

I continued treatment until I recovered. There was no doubt my rib was damaged because I could not run after that treatment, the longest I could play soccer at full breathing strength dwindled to fifteen minutes.

Chuks I. Ndukwe

I studied very hard to catch up with the rest of the class. I borrowed notebooks from my classmates and copied their notes, and I went over all the problems they had solved while I was in the hospital.

We had bunk beds in the dormitory. I slept on the lower bed, so at night, I covered my bed with blankets to avoid breaking the lights-off rule. The campus light went off at nine o'clock every night, and everybody was supposed to sleep after that. I studied by flashlight until midnight or one o'clock every night before going to sleep. My condition turned out to be a blessing in disguise: instead of participating in sports, I was able to focus my energy on studies and social activities. I joined drama and the social evening clubs and was very active in those clubs.

I followed my dormitory prefect, Nnyama, to worship at Anglican Episcopal Church; I was fourteen and looking for a church to worship in. My impression of the Episcopal Cathedral Church on my first Sunday worshipping there was amazement by the magnificence and grandeur of the church. We studied the Bible and prepared for baptism.

One week before my baptism, I had to select a Godfather and a baptismal name from a list containing religious names. I declined and chose an Igbo name—Chukudi—as my baptismal name, and I decided to select Nnyama as my Godfather. Chukudi means, "I believe in God." It represents my solemn belief. On the day of my baptism, ten students from GTC sat in the front pew. It was the most uplifting spiritual experience of my life; I felt like God was right there in the church. During the baptismal ceremony, the priest called the celebrants to the pulpit, as the bishop administered the baptism. Six months later, we received confirmation and had our first communion. As young as I was at the time, I believed I could not have been where I was at the time if I was not safe and secure in God's sacred place. Attending GTC and Mom's transformation from a grieving mother to a woman who went to cities far beyond my village town to attend Christ Apostolic Church meetings and to pray for the sick solidified my belief.

During the second half of the year, we focused on technical exercises, and at the end of the year, we were able to wire different

The Courage To Aspire

types of complicated structures following prescribed rules and regulations. I spent my Christmas holidays at 46 Ulasi Road in Aba with Uncle Emeke Chima and Uncle Okorie Onwuchekwa.

Every time I went to visit Auntie Lucy Okorie, she told me about my niece, I had not met who was a brilliant student at Elelenwa Girl's Secondary School. She gave me the address where her parents lived in Enugu; her dad was a train engineer.

I attended Sunday jump (dance parties for students) every Sunday with one of my best friends, Sam Eke. Sam was very handsome and had a dominant personality. He was a student at a commercial school in Enugu, so we traveled together to and from Enugu most of the time.

One Saturday afternoon, Auntie Lucy sent for me. When I arrived at her house, she was ironing her nurse's uniform. "Ogbuleke, your cousin Comfort arrived yesterday," Auntie Lucy said. "She just left for the cinema on Etche Road. Here's some money for your ticket. Go, hurry up."

She wanted us to be at the cinema together; she would do anything to get us to understand we were related.

"Auntie, I won't recognize her in the theater," "I met her only once, and she didn't even care to say hello. Another thing I have my own money."

"Here, take the money—go," she said and pushed me out.

I told Sam Eke, so we went together. When we got to the theater, she was sitting in the second row with her friends. I could not take the kind of devastating humiliation she would dish out if we got too close, so we sat farther back.

Throughout the show, Sam's eyes were transfixed on her like a hawk; every now and then, I gave him a little nudge. Obviously, Comfort was messing with his head.

"Ogbuleke, I like your sister; in fact, I want to befriend her," Sam said.

"No, I will not let you," I said.

I was aware of how Sam played with girls, so I decided I would not let it happen to Comfort. After the show, I said hello to her.

"I came to the movie because Auntie Lucy gave me money and asked me to meet you here. How long will you be in town?"

"I am going back to Enugu on Saturday," she said.

Sam pinched me from behind, sensing I did not want to introduce him to Comfort.

"Comfort, this is my friend, Sam Eke. Both of us attend school in Enugu. And Sam, meet my cousin Comfort."

"How do you do?" he said.

"How do you do," she responded.

That pleasantry made me so sick I felt like dragging Sam away from Comfort.

"I've got to go; my friends are waiting for me," she said and left.

Sam kept staring at her until she and her two friends went out of sight.

"Ogbuleke, your cousin is beautiful. I will do anything for you if you get us together. I will get you into the Sunday jump free of charge every Sunday."

"Sam, the East Regional government gives me pocket money. I have money for anything I want to do or buy; I don't need your money."

"OK, I won't give you money. Can you take me with you when you go to visit Comfort or let me know when she will come to visit you?" he begged.

"No, go and find another girl. She's out of bounds."

"You stubborn idiot—you can have your sister," he growled and walked away.

A few minutes later, as I was walking home along School Road, Sam caught up with me, and we walked to my uncle's house together.

"Auntie, this is Sam Eke, and Sam, this is my uncle's wife," I said.

"Yes, you are from Amachi. Come in and sit down," she said.

She gave us rice with a blend of red stew. After which, we went to Sunday jump, and two weeks later, we went back to school.

GTC held graduation ceremonies at the beginning of the new school term, and the permanent secretary of the Ministry of Education officiated the occasion. Anyanwu received a scholarship to attend a university in Japan, and Nnyama received a scholarship award to the College of Technology in Enugu. Anyanwu and Nnyama were both school and dormitory prefects, respectively. Both of them were

The Courage To Aspire

residents of my dormitory and students from the electrical department, and I was their aide.

A week later, the principal called me to his office.

"Every year GTC sends two students to GTI—Government Technical Institute, a purely academic institution—to take advanced courses relevant to their field of study," the principal said. "This year, you have been chosen to attend advanced studies at GTI. You will go over there and see the principal for class schedules. On Mondays, Wednesdays, and Fridays, you will attend General Certificate of Education preparatory classes there. Congratulations."

I did not understand what was going on, but I had to comply. The amount of work I did in the beginning at GTC plus additional work at GTI in English, mathematics, advanced mathematics, and physics, was overwhelming but later I got used to it.

In April, I became the secretary of the Social Evening Club. The American Consulate organized the Collegiate Social Club, sponsored by the Nigerian-American Friendship League, so four students represented every high school in Enugu. At GTC, the president and the secretary of the Social Evening Club represented the school by default, so I represented GTC. We debated and held dramatic shows and discussions on current events televised by the Nigerian Broadcasting Corporation (NBC Television) studios in Enugu.

In June, the school staff conducted a General Certificate of Education (GCE) of London University ordinary level examinations, and I was a candidate and passed. In September, I received the GCE ordinary level certificate.

GTC was an institution of highly accelerated studies—two years instead of five—so we were looking forward to graduation already. In November, we took our final examination which lasted for two weeks. Starting from the afternoon the exam ended, we spent every afternoon at the regional capital or Government Secretariat, wandering from one ministry to another—visiting relatives. Every day, visitors from various industries and commercial entities came to interview the graduating students. Seniors attended interviews at the principal's conference room in groups, and nobody said anything about it when they returned to the class.

Chuks I. Ndukwe

I remember seeing a Shell BP bus one day parked in front of the principal's office after lunch and afternoon siesta. Shortly after getting back to class, the principal invited all the seniors to his office, but I was not invited; instead, I sat there alone and languished in despair. When they came back to class, none of them said anything as if they were on a gag order.

At the end of the day, my heart began to race, and my head caught fire with a sudden headache that pounded me all night. I did not bathe that evening, nor did I leave the dormitory for any sports event.

When the bell rang for dinner, I went to the dining hall improperly dressed—casual dress instead of a white shirt, black shorts, and red blazer—so I had to go back to the dormitory and change my clothes before being allowed into the dining hall. I managed to eat, but the food did not have any taste. Awake all night, I closed my eyes a million times, but sleepless until four o'clock in the morning.

I woke up feeling sick, so I did not take part in any morning physical exercise. I reported to the medical center, and my temperature was as high as it could get, I took some pills, ate breakfast, and went to class as usual. On my way back to class after lunch, I saw two cars parked in front of the principal's office. One car had "The Ministry of Education" written on its side, and the second car had "Star Lager Beer" written on the side.

As we sat in the class, the principal sent for our instructor, Mr. Willington. A few minutes later, Miss Donna, the principal's secretary, came into the class. She looked around, and then she took her eyeglasses off and looked again.

"Ogbuleke Ikebie Ndukwe, come to the principal's office," she said.

I got up, shaking, and walked to the principal's office and greeted him as I walked in. "Good afternoon, sir."

"Please sit down," he said.

"This is the student whose records you are reviewing," he told the visitors.

They continued to go through the file in front of them.

I sat scared to death and watched the tall, dark man who seemed to be the leader of the two-man team. He took off his eyeglasses and

The Courage To Aspire

adjusted his tie, and then he looked at me.

"My name is Mba E. Mba. We are from the Ministry of Education," he said. "Every year, the ministry offers scholarships to the College of Technology to two students from this institution with outstanding performance. This year you have been chosen for that award—congratulations," he said.

"Do you have any questions?" The principal asked.

I sat there, motionless and speechless.

"Ogubuleke, do you have any questions?" He asked again.

"No, sir," I said.

"The principal will give you the offer letter; you have until the end of December to accept or decline the offer. Again, congratulations for outstanding performance," Mr. Mba said.

"You can go," the principal said.

I walked out of the principal's office with my instructor by my side.

"You seemed shocked in there," he said. "You will not tell anybody until you have officially accepted the offer."

About an hour later, Miss Donna called me back to the principal's office. I had not quite recovered from the previous shock, so I went back to the office, hoping Mr. Mba had not changed his mind.

There were a few people in the office, maybe four, and they were an entirely new group of people.

"Good afternoon, sir," I greeted.

"This is Ogubuleke. His name is a little hard to pronounce, and these gentlemen are from the Star Brewery Aba. Have a seat," the principal said.

"We understand you are from Aba?" one of the men asked.

"Yes sir, I am from Aba," I answered.

"Which part of Aba?" he asked.

"Forty-six Ulasi Road, sir," I answered.

"Have you visited Star Brewery before?" he asked.

"No sir, but I passed it every time I went home from the train station."

"Would you like to visit us?" he asked.

"Yes, sir, it will be my honor."

"We have gone through every student's record in your department, and we are quite impressed with your achievement, so we have decided to offer you a scholarship to UAC Technical College in Sapele. After graduation, you will join our staff in Aba. How does that sound to you?" he asked.

"Unbelievable sir," I answered.

"You should believe it. Congratulations," one of the men said.

"You can go," the principal said.

When I left the principal's office, I could feel currents of joy flowing throughout my body.

I thought about Mom, Dad, Mr. and Mrs. Okocha, and my uncles and about how happy they would be to hear such a fantastic story. Then I realized I had not accepted the offer yet.

On Thursday the exotic weather had begun to wane, losing its luster and effect on those who luxuriated and soaked themselves in it and dreamed of falling in love in its ever-alluring—but temporary—sensual and seductive presence. I woke up every day eager to do anything and everything, even playing soccer, although my breathing impairment would not allow that. When the breakfast bell went off, I walked to the dining hall with a softer spring in my steps; I believe they called it "swagger."

Approximately thirty minutes after classes began, Miss Donna called me to the office to see the principal.

"Good morning, sir," I saluted.

"Good morning," he said. "I am expecting your letter accepting one of the scholarship awards presented to you earlier this week. You may decline both if you like, but I hope that is not going to be the case. Here are the award brochures for you to review so you can make an informed decision. I suggest you go home and consult with your parents before deciding. Donna will provide you with a voucher; use it to travel to and from home. Be back here on Monday. You can leave right now."

Uncle Emeke Chima was more knowledgeable about colleges; he was educated and a member of the local education committee. Dad depended on him on educational matters as he depended on Dad on traditional issues.

On my way to the train station, I stopped by Auntie Anyanwu's

The Courage To Aspire

house at the railway quarters and told her what had just happened.

"Tell your sister. She is back from school already; they closed last Friday," she said.

Then Comfort came out on her way out, and I told her briefly about the two awards.

"The principal wants me to make a decision soon. Which would you recommend?" I asked.

"The UAC Technical College," she said, and out of the door, she went.

That happened to be my choice for one reason. The Technical College provided the opportunity for a student to spend an equal amount of time in the classroom and in the industry, so at graduation, the student is intellectually ready and technically adept. In contrast, the College of Technology focuses on theoretical principles, leaving the student vulnerable and technically wanting.

I went to the train station and boarded the train. My mind was on how surprised my uncles would be when I get home and broke the news. We arrived at Aba train station at six o'clock in the evening. The streetlights were on everywhere, and the city had never looked more gorgeous.

I took a taxi to 46 Ulasi Road. The family had just had their dinner. Uncle Okorie Onwuchekwa and Anyaele Ochu were lying on their mats in front of the house, chatting and laughing as they did every evening after dinner.

When I got out of the taxi and crossed the little bridge that separated the street from the house, Uncle Okorie sat up.

"Ogbuleke, what is wrong?" he asked.

"Nothing. I came home to talk to you and Uncle Emeke."

He followed me to Uncle Emeke's parlor as he was reading minutes of their Divisional Education Committee meeting. We sat down, and he slowly put the pamphlet upside down and sat up.

"Good evening, uncle," I greeted.

"Ogbuleke, what is wrong?" he asked.

"Nothing," I answered.

I gave him the scholarship award brochures.

"The principal wants me to talk to you and to make a decision before returning to school on Monday," I said.

There was a sigh of relief from everybody.

"You just missed dinner. Let me prepare foo-foo; the soup is still warm," Auntie Ugo said.

After going through the pamphlets, Uncle Emeke explained the contents to Uncle Okorie then they wanted to know my opinion.

"What do you think?" They asked.

"I prefer UAC Technical College."

"Why did you make that choice?" they asked.

"I will gain theoretical and industrial experience at that college; whereas, College of Technology provides theoretical knowledge only."

"We arrived at the same decision," they said.

The following morning, Uncle Anyaele picked me up in his car and took me to the train station, and I boarded the train back to GTC Enugu.

On Monday, I went to the principal's office and gave my acceptance letter to Miss Donna, and after she had typed it, I signed it and handed it to the principal.

"Congratulations. You applied yourself well in this institution. Welcome to the elite club of GTC students who performed above expectations," he said and shook my hand.

I left the office subdued and aware that I was on my way to an institution of higher learning.

Two weeks later, I received a letter from the Star Breweries Aba acknowledging the receipt of my acceptance letter and inviting me to visit the breweries for details of my transition to UAC Technical College.

Chapter 12
Second Step Forward

I don't know where I'm going, but I'm on my way.

~ Carl Sandburg

✳✳✳

On Saturday evening, I arrived home as the Ekoha market was closing, so I relaxed for a while and played with kids before my relatives came returned from the market. Then on Monday, I arrived at Star Breweries at nine o'clock to meet with the accounting manager.

"Ogbuleke, come in and sit down; the manager is waiting for you," Sunday Oje said and directed me to the manager's office.

"Good morning, sir," I greeted him.

"Good morning, please sit down," the manager said.

We went over my financial arrangements, including how much I would be paid on a weekly and monthly basis, how much I wanted my guardian to receive, and the name and address of my guardian.

After deciding all that, he gave me a folder containing the college brochure and the class schedule.

"Go through the brochure. You are required to be at the school a week before classes start for your orientation and room assignment," the manager said "Your monthly allowance will be mailed to you in the second week of every month, and finally, Oje will give you a check for your first month's allowance and your traveling expenses. Contact this office if you have any problems."

I left the manager and stopped by the clerk's office; Sunday Oje and I have not seen each other since he graduated from the commercial high school, so we chatted for a while before he gave me two envelopes containing checks the manager talked about.

"Come visit me when you come home on holidays," he said.

Chuks I. Ndukwe

When I got to my uncles' house, Uncle Anyaele the driver was already waiting to take me home, so I hurried up and put my document away, got in the car, and we took off arriving Alayi at two o'clock and found Mom and Dad were home. After dinner, I explained everything about my hospital admission and my scholarship awards.

"We heard you were hospitalized," Dad said, "I asked your uncles to go and see you, and when they came back I was relieved. How are you feeling?"

"I've been all right since I was discharged from the hospital."

"When are you going to the college in Sapele?" they asked.

"Six weeks from now."

"Will you come home again before you go?" Dad asked.

"No, I would not have the time," I said.

On Saturday morning, Uncle Anyele came home, picked me up, and we drove back to Aba without an additional passenger.

On Sunday, I went to Danfodio Road and visited my brother and my uncle Udensi. There, my uncle had newspapers spread all over the floor as he went through the British soccer league match schedule trying to pick out clubs that would win in their forthcoming matches. So focused as he was, he did not hear me come in. He had played that game for a long time, making lots of money for choosing the winning clubs. I sat down to chat with Dick.

"How long are you going to be in town for the holidays?" he asked.

"I was awarded a scholarship by the Star Breweries Aba to attend UAC Technical College in Sapele, so I will be leaving for Sapele four weeks from now."

"Go to the kitchen and get something to eat," my uncle's wife said.

One week before the beginning of school, I visited the Star Breweries office to inform the financial manager I was leaving for school. Getting there cousin Sunday Oje was chatting with a guest in the lobby, so I sat down and waited for the chat to end before getting his attention.

"Do you want to see me?" he asked.

"Yes and no," I answered.

"How is that?" he asked.

"I want to see Mr. VanHoughsen."

The Courage To Aspire

"OK, you can go into the office," he said.

"Good morning, sir," I greeted.

"Good morning," he replied. "Can I help you?"

"I came to inform you I am leaving for Sapele tomorrow to start school at UAC Technical College."

"Do you have everything you need?" he asked.

"I believe so, sir."

"See Oje before you leave to make sure that you are all set to go," he said.

Before leaving the office, Sunday and I reviewed my file and determined I had everything I needed for my travel.

"OK, I am leaving tomorrow, so I will see you during my next holidays," I said.

After dinner, I informed my uncles that I would be leaving very early in the morning, probably before they woke up and I would write them immediately I arrived at the school; then I bade them good-bye.

"Take some blankets, so you won't sleep on the cement floor again," Uncle Okorie said, reminding me of what happened at GTC.

"I have a key to my room already, and it is fully furnished."

"Safe journey," they said.

I chatted with Auntie Ugo, Teresa, and everybody in the yard and bade them farewell.

Then I joined the kids in the backyard, spread our mats all over the floor, and then we played as usual. I hugged my little niece, Grace, before I went to sleep. I slept well but not without anxiety and fear of the unexpected. At five o'clock, the big bus pulled up at 46 Ulasi Road and blew the horn.

I ran out with my luggage, and the conductor put it inside the luggage compartment. While stepping onto the bus, I saw Auntie Ugo. I waved, took my seat on the bus, and I was on my way to Sapele.

I arrived at Sapele at one o'clock to find passengers and vehicles waiting to be ferried over the river, so we waited until half-past one o'clock, then the barge arrived and transported us over the river. At half-past two o'clock, I arrived at UAC Technical College.

As I was looking for my room number, I realized the college did not have cooking staff, and I was hungry and needed to cook. I asked people for directions to the market and one student from Ghana took me across the street where I bought some rice, onions, pepper, crayfish, melon seed, salt, palm oil, and oha vegetable.

My room was a fully furnished studio with a comfortable bed, cabinet; living room set, and study—but without a stereo set. The kitchen was a huge hall—lined up with stoves; students shared on a first-come-first-use basis.

After cooking dinner, I watched the game of table tennis in the recreation hall, and then I went back to my studio and went to sleep. I slept well, but a little weak and lacked focus when I woke up. I tried to write letters to my uncles, but my writing wasn't scholarly. So I slept all day and all night and regained energy and focus, and I then I wrote letters to my uncles, my parents, and to Sunday Oje, as well as my brother, to inform them of my safe arrival.

On Sunday afternoon, lounging at the recreation hall, the man who had helped me get food items on my arrival came in the recreational hall.

"By the way, my name is Ogbuleke Ikebie Ndukwe," I reminded him. "You helped me yesterday, but I forgot to introduce myself to you. I was so frightened I wouldn't find something to cook that I forgot everything else."

"I am Coujoe A. Kofi. I didn't introduce myself, either—sorry about that," he said.

He wanted to know if I could play table tennis, which I could just a little bit. He picked up two Ping-Pong paddles and offered me one. "Let's see how little," he said.

We warmed up for quite a while, and then we tossed. Kofi served first and went on a rampage, smashing the ball—sending me sideways to chase the ball.

"Easy now Koffi, I just arrived; give me some time to get the hang of it," I said.

"OK, I will be merciful, but my sweetness has a limit," he boasted.

Kofi beat me on one round, twenty-one to sixteen.

"Another round?" he asked.

"Yes, another round," I replied. Then he beat me again.

"This boy is good," I thought.

The Courage To Aspire

We decided to take a walk around the town. We walked along Warri Road until we felt tired, and then we turned around and went back to the campus.

"On whose scholarship are you?" he asked.

"Star Breweries," I said.

"Where is the company located?" he asked.

"Star Breweries is located in Aba, in the Eastern Region of Nigeria," I replied.

"How about you, on whose scholarship are you?" I asked.

"My company is Guinness Breweries in Accra, Ghana."

In the evening, we went to the kitchen and decided to cook at the same time every day. We began to do almost everything together.

The school had a powerful stereo system in the recreation hall, so we spent lots of time in the hall playing Nigerian and Ghanaian music—namely, E. T. Mensa, Rex Lawson, and Osadebe records. Before the school opened, we had indeed become good friends. We spent a considerable amount of time in each other's studio. We cooked and ate together, except when he cooked kenke (dough of pounded corn) which I hated.

One day we went to the soccer field and kicked a ball around. The soccer field was so grassy and green, I could have played on that field forever. I tried running with the ball and did not feel the shortness of breath that had prevented me from playing soccer at GTC. I took Kofi on a dribble around the field a couple of times.

"What should I call you?" he asked. "Ogbuleke is too long."

"Call me Ndukwe if you like," I replied.

Kofi called me Ndukwe, so did everybody else on campus.

"You can play soccer," Kofi said.

"I have a breathing problem," I said.

"I'm sorry about that," he replied.

We went back to the village where I had bought food the last time. When we crossed Warri Road, we saw a short, pretty girl with a sizeable chest and a considerable, round lower backside sitting in front of a beautiful house across the road from the campus.

"Miss, I am looking for yams," I said.

"Come with me," she said.

Chuks I. Ndukwe

We followed her to the rear side of the fenced-in compound.
"Ask my father; he sells yams. His name is Ovie," she said.
"What is your name?" I asked.
"Oro Ovie," she replied.
"My name is Ndukwe, and my friend's name is Kofi. We are starting school across the road on Monday," I said.
"I am glad to meet both of you," she said.
"Likewise," Kofi replied.
"OK, let me get my father," she said.
She went inside the house and came out with her father.
"Father, this is Ndukwe, and this is Kofi. They are looking for yams," she said.
"Are you new students?" he asked.
"Yes, sir," I answered.
"You have chosen a wonderful school. You will be managers when you graduate," he said.
He showed us his collection, and I touched almost every one of the yams before choosing two big yams and four plantains.
"You seem to know how to select good yams," he said.
"Yes sir, Mom taught me," I said. "How much are they all together?"
He hesitated and gave me the price. I paid and then struggled a bit to pick up all my yams and plantains.
"Oro, help these young people to carry their items over to the school," he said.
Oro helped us carry the plantain to the kitchen. Forgetting she was not a visitor, I showed her around the campus, gave her some biscuits, and invited her to come back on Sunday and teach us how to fry plantain.
"I will come after church service," she said.
"Ndukwe, you've got a girlfriend, just like that," Kofi said.
"You are wrong," I said.
Oro came back on Sunday, after church service and knocked on my door.
"Come in," I said.
"This is my studio, and Kofi's is next door. If you want to see me,

The Courage To Aspire

this is my room," I said.

We went to the kitchen but discovered I did not have enough oil to fry the plantain. Not knowing what to do next and unfamiliar with anybody else on the campus yet, we decided to go back to Oro father's house and buy a tin of oil. But we were not entirely comfortable walking along with Oro—we were scared of her father, so we asked her to go home and wait for us. She went back, and thirty minutes later, we went to her house and asked for oil.

Her mother sold a tin—one gallon of palm oil to us, and then we returned to the campus. One hour later Oro came and knocked on my door, then we went to the kitchen. She fried the plantain for us, and I had already cooked rice and stew, so she ate with us. After dinner, she helped me to do the dishes; then we escorted her home. "How is that for slickness?" Kofi said. "I arrived here three days ago, and I haven't met anybody, and you arrived yesterday and already have a girlfriend."

"That's why you haven't met anybody: you are looking for a girl, and I am not looking for anything and if you ask me? I think she is our friend, yours and mine," I said.

"Are you saying that if she comes to visit you, and you are alone in your room, nothing will happen?" Kofi asked.

"First of all, you and I are always together, so the chance of her visiting when I am alone is very slim. Second, if she comes, I will call you over. Did you see how mean-looking her father is?"

"He may not be that mean," Kofi said.

"On the other hand, he might be worse than he looks," I countered.

✹ ✹ ✹

The school began on Monday with orientation for the incoming students; the returning students started classes immediately. Our orientation lasted for four hours through the morning session.

We began classes in the afternoon. The school library has every book the students needed, and all we had to do was pick books from the library at the beginning of every class.

Classes were very intense. My electrical engineering instructor, Mr. Willington, was a very experienced electrical engineer. Unlike other instructors, his lectures did not last for more than one hour. He taught basic principles and derivation of electrical engineering formulas, and the rest was up to us. Kofi and I did our assignments on every subject in the classroom, except electrical engineering; we did everything electrical in our studios.

I studied, as I had never done before, making sure I covered the topic of every lesson before class began. We solved as many problems as we could well beyond the regular assignment. Mr. Willington would correct the work and pass out the notebooks at the beginning of each lecture. Occasionally he would pick out the most nagging problems for us to tackle together in the class.

In June freshman students went back to the companies that awarded them scholarships, so I went back to the Star Breweries Aba—brewer of Star lager beer for my practical experience. I worked with the engineers and the technical staff. I followed the electrical foreman, Mr. Olatunde Olayemi, around to learn how to inspect, diagnose, and repair electrical machines and motors. One day, I went to the yeast fermentation room. Before the engineers had completed their work on the machine, I passed out in the room and woke up in the hospital and found Uncle Emeke Chima and Uncle Okorie Onwuchekwa sitting on my bed.

"Ogbuleke, do you know where you are?" they asked.

"No, why am I here?" I asked.

"The doctor will tell you," they said.

Suddenly, the doctor walked in. "Good, you are awake. I did not think you would wake up so soon. Do you know why you are not at work?" he asked.

"No, sir," I answered.

"Do you remember the last place you went to in the breweries?" he asked.

"Yes, sir. I went to the yeast fermentation room with the electrical engineers to inspect an electrical machine, and I helped them to turn the machine off before disconnecting it. That's the last thing I remember."

"That's correct," the doctor said. "You do not have any tolerance for alcohol, so you should never drink or inhale alcohol. Again, you have zero tolerance for alcohol. We will keep you in the ward for two hours and detoxify you, and then you will be free to go home."

The Courage To Aspire

My visitors stayed for a while and left the hospital. Later, Mr. Olatunde came to the hospital and stayed for a while with me.

"Did you drink any beer?" he asked.

"No, sir, I did not," I replied.

"When you left me in the workshop, where did you go before you went to the fermentation room?" he asked.

"I went straight to the fermentation room with the engineers who were working in the room."

"Rumor is going around that you got drunk in the bottling room."

"I've not been to the bottling room or near the conveyor today," I said.

"You don't have to come to work tomorrow if you don't feel good," Mr. Olatunde said.

Although I had not begun to drink alcohol—everybody in my family drinks, and they never got sick. I worried about the possibility of losing my scholarship due to alcohol intolerance and about how I would work at a place I would get sick doing my job. It came to me; some people wore masks when they worked in some areas—ah! That ought to be the solution.

I left the hospital and went home, and my uncles were still in the market, and by the time they came home, I was feeling well or normal again like my usual self.

***

On the second Saturday of January, I arrived at the campus just as the graduating students were going back to start work as supervisors in their respective companies. Oro helped me stock up our pantry before Kofi arrived.

A week after I had returned to school, the principal gave me an application form for the Full Technological Certificate, (advanced technical certificate) examination conducted by the City and Guilds of London Institute. Three months later, I received a full technological certificate in electrical engineering.

When classes resumed, we began to cover all phases of electrical generations and transmission. We immersed ourselves in the quiet waters of studies, with extracurricular activities relegated to weekend pass time. In June, we took our final exam before going back to our respective companies for practical experience.

At the Star Breweries, I handled all aspects of the technical work, dismantling motors, machines; repairing, reassembling, and testing their functionality. By December, I was adept in all aspects of the brewery's electrical system. The engineers watched me as I conducted inspections and tests, and wrote reports on every work I did. The chief engineer came to my office a few times and asked me questions about different machines and their various phases of operation. On each occasion, I answered his questions with math, vectors, and graphs.

At the end of the year, I went back to school to attend my graduation ceremony. After the ceremony, Kofi and I spent a week together before we parted company.

When I arrived at Star Breweries to begin work, Star Brewery provided me with a chalet at the European quarters; I declined because at sixteen I was too young to live there; moreover, it would have been too far from my uncles' house. Finally, they rented a flat for me at 57 Milverton Avenue, very close to the movie theater and the motor park and within walking distance of the brewery.

When I reported to the personnel office on Monday of the second week of January, I started work immediately as the supervisor of the electrical department. My office was located very close to the workshop, and Mr. Olatunde's desk was in the workshop outside my office. Shortly after the chief engineer announced my position and Mr. Olatunde went crazy. He paced back and forth; went outside and came back. Then later, I posted the work schedule and handed work orders to him.

He threw the papers on the floor, went to the bottling room, and stayed there until the end of the day. The following morning, the chief engineer came in the workshop and saw the papers on the floor, picked them up and walked straight into my office and asked why the work orders were on the floor.

"Mr. Olatunde threw them on the floor to protest my position as his supervisor," I said.

He called Mr. Olatunde to his office and resolved the matter.

Chapter 13
The Wrong Way To Start

The worst part of success is trying to find someone who is happy for you.

~ Bette Midler

My first week working as a supervisor at the Star Breweries Aba was not the happy and exciting beginning of my professional life I had expected. I had hoped it would be a time for me to prove to the company that the money they had spent to educate me was worth the investment but instead misdirected anger and petty jealousy reigned. Every morning when I got to work, I found substances with offensive odors in my office. I was unafraid and calm and treated it as a joke—dismissing its possible effect on my life.

One morning I opened my drawer and found a little package wrapped with lace and tiny strings and covered with blood, eggshells, and a yellow substance. I waited until everybody had arrived at the workshop, and then I held the package up for everybody to see.

"My name is Ogbuleke Ikebie Ndukwe; I am from Amaigwu Amankalu Alayi in Bende Division," I said. "I am not afraid of voodoo or nsi or whatever it's called in Yoruba or Hausa. Whoever sprinkles dirt around my desk and shoves this thing in my drawer must stop doing so. It will not work." I smashed it on the floor.

"The foreman, Mr. Olatunde, is doing it. He said that you are too young to boss him around," one of the technicians said.

Mr. Olatunde continued to make a fool of himself, and it did not bother me anymore. However, the environment had become toxic, and workers are looking at each other with suspicion. I was feeling extremely uncomfortable working in that kind of atmosphere, so I told my uncles about it. Uncle Emeke wanted to report the matter to the management, but I persuaded him not to.

On Monday morning I got to my office, and two workers had arrived before me. Usually, I tried to be the first person to get to the shop, but that day they beat me. They were standing in front of my office with their hands folded. When I got to the office door, I found a disgusting black powder, eggshells, and a glittering yellow substance like rat poison with an offensive odor smeared on my door and on the floor. I left it there and went home in a taxi, as Uncle Emeke was getting ready to go to the market.

"Uncle, I can't take it anymore! I cannot work at the breweries," I growled.

"What are you going to do?" he asked. "They spent lots of money to train you, and I will not let that Yoruba man drive you out of your job. You are the first black man to work there as a supervisor. Come on; follow me."

"Uncle, where are we going?" I asked.

"We are going to breweries. I'd like to speak to the manager and to that Olatunde," he said and started to walk out of the house with his shirt not quite fully buttoned up.

"Uncle, I don't want to work there any longer," I repeated.

"Ogbuleke, I've always admired your decisions, but this time your behavior is childish, and you are completely wrong," he said. "If you leave that company, they will come after all of us; do you understand that?" I was quite aware my uncle meant well by trying to inject fear into my mind, but the problem was that I had made up my mind, and at that time there was nothing that could change it. I was neither afraid of the voodoo nor Olatunde. I simply did not want to start my professional life working in an atmosphere tainted with hostility, petty jealousy, and ignorance.

While we were standing in front of the house arguing, a thought came to mind spontaneously.

"Uncle, if anybody comes here to look for me," I said, "tell them I went to work this morning and I haven't come home since then and that

The Courage To Aspire

you were preparing to go to the breweries to find out what was holding me from coming home."

"Where will you be hiding?" he asked.

"I am going to Port Harcourt to look for work at the Nigerian Refineries."

"Are you sure you know what you are doing?"

"I am not sure, but I have no choice," I answered.

I put enough money in my pocket for a round-trip bus fare, and then I took off. I boarded the bus at nine-thirty in the morning. Got to the refineries at Eleme and went straight to the chief engineer's office as his secretary was trying to sit down with a cup of coffee in her hand; I pulled the chair out for her to sit down.

"Good morning, ma'am, my name is Ogbuleke Ikebie Ndukwe. I want to see the chief engineer; I am from Star Breweries Aba," I said, holding my diplomas and my full technological certificate in electrical engineering in my hand.

"Sir, there is a young man from Star Breweries in the office, and he wants to see you," she told the chief engineer.

"Show him in," he said.

I walked into the office boldly looking confident.

"Good morning, sir," I greeted him.

"Good morning, what brought you here?" he asked.

I handed my credentials to him and explained to him what I was going through as a young man trying to enter the workforce.

"Sit down," he said.

He looked over the papers I handed him a couple of times, and then he called his secretary.

"Abby, tell Mr. Chijioke and Ahuchogu to come to my office," he said.

"When did you receive your full tech certificate?" he asked.

"Last year sir," I replied.

"Which college did you attend in England?" he asked.

"I've never been to England," I replied.

"Oh, I see you just graduated from UAC Tech. I know the principal—Mr. Willington. Am I right?" he asked.

"You are right sir," I said.

Chuks I. Ndukwe

While we were waiting for the two people he had sent for, he explained the structure of the management staff and the division of authority among them to me.

"It takes three managers to hire somebody of supervisory level and up—or unanimous four—as the case may be," he said. "For every position, we have a European and a Nigerian, so we have three Nigerian engineers: Mr. Chijioke, mechanical; Mr. Ahuchogu, instruments; and Mr. Njoku, electrical. We have not been able to agree on any European engineer, so we have three openings for European engineers and one opening for a Nigerian supervisor. All these three engineers and I—or two of them and I—have to agree before we can hire a supervisor or engineer. I would like you to speak with these gentlemen, and then I will give you my opinion."

Mr. Ahuchogu was the first person to come to the chief engineer's office.

"Sorry, I had an emergency in the control room," he said.

"Do you have time to speak with Mr. Ndukwe? He is looking for the position of supervisor," he said and handed my papers to him.

"Definitely, I can spare few minutes," Mr. Ahuchogu said.

I followed him to his office. He went to the restroom, washed his hands, came back to his office, and closed the door.

"Have a seat. My name is Anthony Ahuchogu, and I am the instrument engineer," he said.

"My name is Ogbuleke Ikebie Ndukwe. I started work at the Star Breweries two weeks ago as an electrical supervisor," "but the environment became really toxic in a short time, so I came here to look for a job."

"Tell me what happened," he said.

I explained everything that had happened in the short two weeks, I worked at the breweries.

"That's a shame. Believe it or not, I worked at the breweries before joining the refineries," Mr. Ahuchogu said. "I know Mr. Olatunde; he's been there since the company started operation. I am from Ngwa, not too far from the breweries. It would have been easy if you had any experience."

"Sir, my school, is a sandwich educational institution, so I have

The Courage To Aspire

enough industrial experience in addition to my technical experience at GTC," I replied.

"Have you used any instruments to troubleshoot electrical problems?" he asked.

"Yes, sir. I am adept in oscilloscopes and multimeters, and I can solder and repair any electrical equipment," I said.

"Have you worked with any switchgear?" he asked.

"Yes sir, I am conversant with Baldwin and Locksmith switch gears," I said.

"What is the difference between them?" he asked.

"Baldwin's contacts are immersed in nonconductive cooling oil, whereas Locksmith switchgear has dry contact," I answered.

"Do you know the difference between domestic and industrial electrical power systems, and if so, explain."

"Domestic power, two hundred forty volts, is derived from a single phase of the star three-phase electrical generator," I said and illustrated the structure with graphs and a vector diagram. "And industrial power, level four hundred volts, is from a three-phase generator, usually of delta formation." I again illustrated it with drawing and vector.

"I have no other questions. I will send you back to Mr. Summerlin," he said.

Then he took me over to Mr. Chijioke's office and gave my papers to him.

"Could you have few words with Mr. Ndukwe?" he said.

"Good morning, sir. My name is Ogbuleke Ikebie Ndukwe."

"Good morning. I am Christopher Chijioke. I'm a mechanical engineer. Do sit down."

He went over my papers a few times, and then he walked out of the office and chatted with Mr. Ahuchogu before coming back to his office. "I am quite impressed. Have you met with Mr. Njoku?" he asked.

"No, sir, I have not."

"OK, I will see you after meeting with him." He walked me back to Mr. Summerlin's office, and both of them chatted outside the office. When he came back to the office, he wanted me to see Mr. Njoku, so Miss Abby escorted me over to Mr. Njoku's office, and I gave him my papers. He glanced over the sheets of paper and put them aside on his table.

"I am not looking for an electrical supervisor. I already have Akwaja, and he is terrific. I don't know why she brought you to me," he said.

"The chief engineer asked me to see you," I said.

"Well, you've seen me, and my answer is no," he repeated.

I left his office with my papers, went back to Mr. Summerlin's office, and told him what had transpired in Mr. Njoku's office.

"It's not important," he said. "That's why I sent you there last. We have already decided to hire you, but your age is troubling. However, if you can go home and have your father execute an affidavit of a declaration of date of birth, we will consider you favorably."

Then he gave me an envelope to give to Dad.

"Thank you, sir. I will be back," I said.

I took a bus right away to Port Harcourt road and another bus to Aba. Dad was not educated; he would not understand what date of birth meant. However, Uncle Emeke was educated—he knows the statutory requirements for employment—so I went to the city hall with him. He wrote the declaration by hand, signed it, and had it stamped, dated, and signed by the city-hall clerk. Then I snatched it from him and ran to Asa Road. I took a bus back to the refinery and handed the affidavit to Mr. Summerlin. Finally, he shook my hand.

"Congratulations. I look forward to seeing you on Monday," he said.

Miss Abby gave me some papers to fill out, and after filling out the papers, she went over every one of them.

"I don't want the stupid people in Lagos to send any of these papers back; they seem to enjoy sending things back," she complained.

I waited for a bus at the gate. Luckily, Mr. Ahuchogu saw me as he drove through the gate on his way home. Then he stopped and signaled me to get in his car.

"I will take you to Port Harcourt Road, and then you can take the bus home," he said. "Congratulations! Do not worry about Mr. Njoku; you will be under my supervision when you start on Monday. You can come to work from Aba until you find a flat like I did when I started working here."

The Courage To Aspire

He dropped me off at the Port Harcourt Road bus stop. Then I waited for a bus until a Peugeot 404 returning to Aba stopped, then I jumped in and returned to Aba before my uncle came home in the evening.

When Uncle Emeke came home, he seemed upset.

"Why is the front door unlocked? I told you, people, to keep it locked," he said.

"I got the job," I said and gave him my employment papers.

"I am proud of you. At least you do not have to worry about alcohol getting you sick. Do not tell anybody. I will tell Uncle Okorie, and we will tell everybody when it is safe to do so."

On Tuesday, I went back to Port Harcourt to look for a flat. The first area I stopped by was Diobu. I turned at Ikwere Road, found a vacant room for rent, and asked for the owner, and he came out of the drugstore on the ground floor of the three-story building.

"Sir, I am looking for a flat," I said.

"The flats are occupied; what I have is a room," he said.

"'I would like to look at it," I said.

He took me around the corner to the room by the staircase. I looked around, and there wasn't really much to see in a one-room apartment.

"I'll take it," I said.

I gave the landlord, Mr. Onwumere, an advance to hold the room for me, and then I went home in the evening. On Friday, I went to my flat on Milverton Avenue and moved my belongings to 46 Ulasi Road; I packed all night. On Saturday morning, I found a kaikai bus. The driver drove the van to Ulasi Road and loaded my things, and then I left Aba for Port Harcourt.

On our way to Port Harcourt—on January 15, 1966, just as we cleared Aba Township—we heard on the radio that a group of soldiers had overthrown the federal government. They mentioned the names of the soldiers who organized the coup: Nzegwu, Obasanjo, etc. The news was so confusing; the report said the soldiers had taken over the government, and a few minutes later, the radio announced they had handed the government to another senior military officer.

At that time, Nigeria comprised of three regions: the Northern Region, dominated by Muslims—the Hausa tribe; the Eastern Region, dominated by Christians—the Ibo tribe; and the Western Region, dominated by Christians—the Yoruba tribe. Before the coup, Abubakar Tafawa Balewa, Dr. Nnamdi Azikiwe, and Chief Obafemi Awolowo represented the three regions in the federal government.

When I arrived in Diobu in the afternoon, I rented a truck and moved my luggage to 21 Owerri Road. I hooked up my stereo system and glued myself to the radio as the news came fast and furious, changing by the minute.

Later in the evening, I went to the market and bought groceries and a kerosene stove. Every tenant cooked in the same kitchen, so there were three cooking fireplaces. While I was setting up my cooking stove, a man came to the kitchen.

"My name is Kanu N. Kanu, and I am from Ohafia," he said.

"My name is Ogbuleke Ikebie Ndukwe, and I am from Alayi," I replied.

"I am glad to meet you," he said.

"So am I," I said.

"You seem new."

"Yes, I arrived this afternoon."

"Come upstairs after dinner; I live in the second flat."

After dinner, I went upstairs, and his door was open with a curtain hanging down to prevent people from looking directly into his living room. We listened to the news until late at night, and then I decided to go to bed.

"Tomorrow is Saturday, and the night is still young—relax," he said.

"You are right, but I have to go and set my bed up," I said.

As I was setting my bed up, Mr. Kanu called, "ND, come upstairs quickly; the news is breaking again."

I went to his flat, and the radio was listing the names of government officials who were gunned down during the coup—namely, Prime Minister Abubakar Tafawa Balewa, the premier of the Northern Region; Ahmadu Bello, Chief Akintola, premier of the Western Region; and Chief Festus Okotieboh, the federal finance minister.

"Right then, Aguiyi Ironsi, the top military commander, had been appointed the supreme commander of the military government," the

The Courage To Aspire

radio broadcast.

We were stunned, unaware of the ramifications of the developing events. We lay on Mr. Kanu's couch and fell asleep, overcome by the gravity of the situation. When we woke up, it was late at night.

"There have been numerous coups in different parts of the world, and it never ended well. I think we are in trouble," Mr. Kanu said.

"What are you talking about?" I asked, not knowing anything about the world. "I have to go to sleep."

"Goodnight."

✻ ✻ ✻

When I arrived at the refinery on Monday, I went straight to the electrical workshop. We had another supervisor—a white man, Mr. John Chamberlin. His job was to inspect the electrical systems, write work orders for the repairs, and give the work order to Mr. Njoku. When he came to the workshop that morning, he walked straight to me and asked me to follow him to the substation.

"Mr. Summerlin does not get along with Mr. Njoku. He thinks he's an idiot," he said. "He wants me to work closely with you, and very likely Mr. Ahuchogu will be your actual manager, so don't mind Mr. Njoku's attitude."

When we got to the substation, I looked around and all the switchgear were Baldwin's switches.

"These are wonderful switches," I said.

"How do you know about Baldwin switches?" he asked.

"I have operated, dismantled, and assembled them several times," I said.

"OK, when we inspect the switches, what should we be looking for?" he asked

"The condition of the cooling oil and how oxidized the switching blades are," I said.

"That's fantastic; so now I can go on vacation when I want," he said.

"Why do you say that?" I asked.

"Every time I wanted to go on vacation, Mr. Summerlin had to get somebody from Kent in England to come over here and relieve me," he said, "but now you can do my job. So there will be no need to fly somebody here from England."

We inspected the oil, and it was still functionally sound. I disconnected the switchblades and cleaned them with sandpaper, and then I wheeled them back in place and tested them.

"Looks good," I said.

"Let's go and see the boss," he said.

"No, you go alone; that's your job," I said.

"Remember, we are a team, and he'd love to know what we did together.

When we got to Mr. Summerlin's office, he was with Mr. Ahuchogu, discussing some relay issues in the control room.

"How are the switches?" he asked.

"Tell Mr. Summerlin about our inspection at the substation," Mr. Chamberlain said.

"Let's hear it," Mr. Summerlin said.

"Sir, the switches are sound," I said.

"OK, I want the two of you to go with Mr. Ahuchogu and check the signaling relay in the control room. Ndukwe, I want to see you in my office after lunch," Mr. Summerlin said.

So we followed Mr. Ahuchogu to the control room to check the relay. It was not accessible, therefore I climbed up the panel, disconnected it, and took it to the workshop.

We applied power to it, and it worked, so I requested the assistance of one of the electricians. Mr. Ahuchogu assigned Francis Okogbuo as my aide, so he followed me to the control room, and we traced the fault to the control panel. We replaced the push button, and the problem was resolved. After lunch, I went to see Mr. Summerlin, afraid, thinking I had done something wrong. I knocked on the door.

"Come in, Mr. Ndukwe," Miss Abby said. "Sir, Ndukwe is here."

"Show him in," he said.

"Sir, I am here as you requested," I said.

"I want to know: did John put you up to what you said about the inspection you did at the substation?" he asked.

"No, sir. I told him I was familiar with Baldwin switches, then he

The Courage To Aspire

challenged me to prove it. So I conducted the inspection myself."

"I'd like you to write the test report and give it to Miss Abby," Mr. Summerlin said.

After I had written the report, Mr. Ahuchogu reviewed it before I gave it to Miss Abby. The following morning, Mr. Summerlin sent for me. As I was coming out of the workshop, he walked into the workshop with Mr. Ahuchogu and Mr. Njoku.

"Listen up, everybody. Mr. Ndukwe is the new electrical supervisor," he announced. "He will work with John on special assignments, and he will also supervise general electrical work when necessary." "That report was fantastic," he said to me as he was leaving the workshop.

I went to John's office and told him it was official; we would be working together. Every week, I checked designated junction boxes on the oil pipeline with Francis to verify the integrity of the silica gel—the substance that absorbs moisture inside the pipe. We replaced the gel when the original color changed. This operation went from the refinery's gate all the way to Okarika jetty, where ships docked. One day, we were inspecting one of the junction boxes when Francis sent me to buy biscuits for the electricians who were changing the gel.

Although I was their supervisor, I did errands for them because they were much older than I was. There was a little store across the street, so I went in to look for biscuits and sweets. A girl was sitting behind the counter, reading the novel *Young Love*. I had read it myself several times before.

"That is a nasty novel," I said.

"Have you read it?" she asked.

"It was authored by a nineteen-year-old girl by the name of Jenny, and it's all about her first boyfriend, Francis, and how she lost her virginity."

"OK, recite one passage in the novel," she demanded.

"One page: 'Francis, oh! Francis, how little did he know I was letting him into a world nobody has ever been before?' "

"One more passage?" she said.

I asked her to show me her collection of biscuits and sweets. She put some on the counter, and as she turned to get some more, I saw

"Okarika Grammar School" on her shirt.

"Are you a student at Okarika Grammar School?" I asked.

"One more passage from the novel; then I will tell you my school," she said.

"Another page: 'There's nothing that rends the heart that mars progress and destroys hope as treachery and deceit by those we love most.' "

"OK, now tell me your school," I demanded.

"Enuda Girls," she said.

"Are you talking about Enuda Girls in Abariba?" I asked.

"Yes, I am."

"I am from Alayi; you pass my town before getting to your school," I said.

"Why did you read that novel? Are you a virgin?" she asked.

"It's not your business," I said.

She bagged six Tofi chocolate bars, six graham crackers, and one pack of groundnut. I paid for my items, and before I left the store, I wrote my name, and address on a paper, and gave it to her.

"You can write to me when you get back to school or visit me when you come home on holidays. I hope you will not play hard to get," I said.

"Look at the wastebasket; that's where I throw such paper," she said.

"Look, if you are going to throw my address away," I said, "don't throw it in the trash. Instead, throw it outside, so my luck and charm will follow me."

I left the store without looking back; I really did not care what she did with my paper.

※※※

On Monday morning, Miss Abby came to my office. "Mr. Ndukwe, Mr. Summerlin, wants you in his office."

"I think I am in trouble," I said to John.

I went to Mr. Summerlin's office, and three white men were sitting on the couch.

"This is my new supervisor, Mr. Ndukwe. You will be working with him," he told them. "These electrical engineers are from BP Petroleum in Kent, England. You will assist them in their technical audit."

"I will be glad to assist in any way as needed," I replied.

"OK, then," he said.

I followed the three engineers around the electrical systems, carrying the refinery blueprint and the electrical wiring schematics. We went from one substation to another. At every station, I performed the actual inspections, and the visitors documented the results. We checked the junction boxes as well.

After the first inspection, I became very familiar with every aspect of the electrical system at the Eleme Refinery. I kept copies of the blueprints and the schematics in case I was called upon to perform the inspections by myself or something catastrophic happened in the electrical system that required detailed analysis and troubleshooting.

***

One day after work, I was relaxing in my bed, when my younger brother, Anyele, arrived with a young woman—about fourteen.

"Mom wants her to live with you," Anyele said. "Her name is Catherine. She is our brother's prospective wife; she is not supposed to know. Give me money for the bus," he said, "I am going back now." (It was customary for girls to live with any member of her prospective husband's relatives until the family felt that she was right for their son). Mom had confidence in my ability not only to determine if she was right for my brother but to take care of her and make her feel comfortable.

"Stay till tomorrow," I begged Anyele. "I am going upstairs. Change your clothes and take a shower; I'll be back," I said, after showing them the bathroom.

I went to Mr. Kanu's flat to think. I was living in one room, and the girl needed privacy. I could have sent her back, but I thought it was an opportunity for me to prove to Mom that I was the son she had taught me to be.

Chuks I. Ndukwe

"Buy a curtain and hang it across the room so you can have privacy," Mr. Kanu said.

I took a bus to the market and bought a beautiful curtain, and then I hung it across the room. When I went to the kitchen to cook, Cathy and Anyele came to the kitchen, and the three of us cooked together.

The following morning, I gave Anyele his bus fare and pocket money before I went to work.

"I gained admission to Ngwa High School Aba," Anyele said, "I will come back for my tuition fees and money for my uniform and books."

"Congratulations," I said and hugged him.

He came back a few weeks later and gave me a sheet of paper showing his financial needs for the high school: school fees, boarding, books, and other materials. So I gave him the amount stipulated in the brochure.

One day soon afterwards, when I came home from work, Cathy was lying on the floor in a pool of blood crying. I panicked, and I did not know what to do. I could not pick her up; she was my brother's wife, and I did not want to touch her for the same reason.

"Cathy, what happened? Did you cut yourself?" I asked.

"I don't know what happened. I'm bleeding between my legs," Cathy said.

I remembered a similar incident from primary school.

"Cathy, I will be right back," I said.

I went to the drugstore right in front of the building. The owner was a chemist who had been educated in America. I asked her for help, and she gave me pads and special underwear. I bought six of each. Then I ran to the bookstore and bought a book—menstruation cycles and how to manage it. I showed the book to the chemist, and she approved of it. Then I gave it to Cathy and showed her how to put the pads on. She went to the bathroom to change, and then I mopped the floor and took her out shopping. When we came home in the evening, she was feeling better—confident and happy again. I took her to the drugstore and introduced her to the chemist, so she could help her when she needed feminine advice.

One evening, on July 29, 1966, just after dinner, news broke that

Gowon and other military officers had overthrown Aguiyi Ironsi's government. The coup organizers had killed Aguiyi Ironsi during a visit to Ibadan, the capital city of the Western Region of Nigeria. As in the previous coup, news came over the radio fast-changing every hour—so I went up to Mr. Kanu's flat. He seemed to have a better insight into what was happening.

"Didn't I tell you that coups never end well?" he asked.

"You are right," I said.

A few days later, the supreme military council appointed Colonel Gowon as the supreme leader and head of state of the military government of Nigeria. The second coup was now complete, and the federal government was now firmly in the hands of the Hausas—the Muslims and nobody could predict how the whole ordeal would end.

***

On Saturday, January 14, 1967, I was playing ticktacktoe with Cathy when somebody knocked on the door. Cathy opened the door, and there was the girl I had met at the store by the refinery.

"Hello. Come in please," I said.

"Sorry, I didn't introduce myself to you the day we met," I said. "My name is Ogbuleke Ikebie Ndukwe."

"Same, my name is Fortune Darling Waribere," she said.

"This is my sister, Cathy D. Ndukwe," I told Fortune, "Cathy, this is my friend."

"Your sister is beautiful," she said.

"Please have a seat."

"Are you happy I did not throw away the note you gave me?" she asked.

"Yes, that was very nice of you," I said.

I was playing favorite classical records by Jim Reeves and Nat King Cole—when she arrived and then I sent Cathy to the store to buy biscuits and orange Fanta for the guest.

Fortune stayed for quite a while; she liked my choice of music and the stereo system. However, she wondered why I did not rent a flat; I assured her I'd rent one as soon as one became vacant.

"What's your job at the refinery?" she asked.
"I am an electrical supervisor," I replied.
"Where did you attend school?" she asked.
"I graduated from UAC Technical College, Sapele," I explained.

I could tell she liked Cathy from the way they played together and walked around the block, and Fortune bought some sweets for her. When Fortune decided to go home, Cathy and I escorted her to the bus stop and waited with her until the bus arrived. Then I paid the fare, and she got on the bus and waved.

"I will see you again before I go back to school," she said.
"Please do," I said.

I was happy to see Fortune. She was a gorgeous girl, and I had not actually expected her to write or visit me.

When I arrived at the refinery on Monday, I went straight to Francis.

"She visited; I mean she actually came to my room," I told him.
"Who visited?" he asked.
"That girl I met at the store when we were checking silica gel at the pipeline," I said.
"You're lying," he said.
"We played records, and she liked my sister—I was pretending Cathy was my sister—and she said that she will visit again before she goes back to school."
"You hit a gold mine," Francis said.

Fortune visited again on Sunday before the beginning of school. When she knocked on the door, Cathy knew she was the person knocking on the door.

"Brother, its Fortune," she said.
"Open the door, and let her in," I said.
"Kate, Kate." Fortune greeted Cathy by her nickname.

We spent the whole day with Fortune, and she helped Cathy cook rice and stew. She was an excellent cook.

When she decided to go home in the evening, I gave her pocket money. She took it, but then she gave it back to me. At first, I thought the amount wasn't enough, so I increased it.

The Courage To Aspire

"I don't want you to give me any money. My parents give me enough money, so I have plenty of spending money," she explained.

It was reassuring she refused the money; at that time, rumor had it that high-school girls pursued wealthy men to milk them. I could tell from her actions that she was a decent person. When she decided to go home, Cathy and I escorted her to the bus stop. When the bus arrived, we hugged. She hugged Cathy and then she boarded the bus.

"Write me when you get to school" I said.

"I will; bye-bye," she said.

"Bye-bye," we responded.

Chapter 14
Nigeria-Biafra War

The true soldier fights not because he hates what is in front of him, but because he loves what is behind him.

~ G.K. Chesterton

The atmosphere in Nigeria had become tense as the TV-televised incidents of Ibos being killed and maimed by Muslims in the northern region—and their bodies piled up like a pyramid for the Ibos to see—it was hard to watch. Consequently, on May 30, 1967, the governor of the Eastern Region, Lieutenant Colonel Emeka Odumegwu Ojukwu declared the region the Independent Republic of Biafra to give the Ibo people the legal right to defend themselves.

Consequently, the unity and uneasy peace that held Nigeria together began to unravel. In a short time, news came that the northern Hausa soldiers were amassing at the border to march southwards and exterminate the Ibo tribe. In Enugu, the new Biafran head of state, Lieutenant Colonel Emeka Odumegwu Ojukwu, appealed to Ibos to enlist in the Biafra military to raise a force large enough to stand up against the federal troops.

Young people, the Ibos, Ijaws, and the Efiks rushed to Enugu to enlist in the army in response to the head of state's plea—especially university and college graduates, like me, out of a sense of patriotism and self-defense.

When I arrived at the recruiting center, the recruiting officer sent me back to the refinery because I was performing an essential service. At the refinery, relationships strained. John did not like Ojukwu's action; he called him an idiot, so I cursed him out and vehemently objected to his assertions, and we could not really work together anymore.

On July 6, 1967, Gowon declared war on Biafra. Then I sent Cathy

The Courage To Aspire

home.

Two weeks later, Odumegwu Ojukwu promulgated an edict expatriating white people from Biafra. Before the white engineers departed, they dismantled the electrical system and turned the plant off.

Then Ojukwu flew into the refinery and summoned everybody to the conference room. He played a recording of a discussion he had had with the president of BP of London. In their conversation, the president of BP warned Ojukwu against his edict and expatriation of the BP engineers and stated that Biafrans did not have the skill, intelligence, knowledge, and expertise to run and operate the refinery.

"Was he correct?" he asked.

"Noooooooooh," we yelled.

"I want to know, do you have the skill, the knowledge, the intelligence and the expertise to restart this refinery and run it as Biafrans?" he asked

"Yeaaaaaaaaaah!" we shouted.

"OK then, this refinery must be up and running within forty-eight hours from now," he ordered. "You must do all you can to get it back in full operation. I have provided your management with a shortwave transceiver; let me know when petrol starts to flow again." Then he boarded his helicopter and glided away.

After the head of states departure, Mr. Chijioke gathered the engineers and the supervisors together, but Mr. Njoku was missing.

"Can we get the electrical system back in operation?" he asked.

There was no answer. I did not want to volunteer until Mr. Njoku, or Akwaja had said something. We waited and looked for Mr. Njoku, and then Mr. Ahuchogu asked me if I was willing to take on the responsibility of restoring the electrical system to its fullest functionalities.

"I will assist you," he said.

"Yes, sir, I can do it," I reassured him.

It was apparent that the major problem was electrical power. If that got resolved, everything else would be much easier. So I went to work; I isolated every substation and turned the switches off. Then I went around the complex with Mr. Ahuchogu and the electricians, including Akwaja, and switched all machines, pumps, and motors off. I began to inspect and test every substation. With all four substations thoroughly inspected, checked, and tested, I began to turn them on, one at a time until the entire refinery lit up as if nothing had ever happened.

Mr. Chijioke was checking all the mechanical structures in parallel, so when he completed the inspection of the mechanical structure, Mr. Essien went in with his operations people. When he turned the heater on, the entire refinery began to shake as if it was getting ready to explode. So he turned the system off and allowed the pipe network to cool to a safe temperature. With the aid of the piping blueprint, Mr. Chijioke, managers, and supervisors, began to inspect every tank and every column through the drainage valves.

After a long and agonizing traversing of the refinery complex, they discovered that the white engineers had filled the oil feeder tanks with water and had emptied the cooling tower, hence the system was boiling. In the control room, request for our progress was coming in from The Head of State's office. It was approaching thirty-six hours, with only twelve hours to go before we broke the edict. We had not gone home nor taken a break, but we were not feeling tired or even hungry. After draining the water, the operators refilled the feeder tanks with crude oil and the cooling tower with water and restarted the operation. We gathered around the control panel and watched as each meter began to register the state of the columns it was monitoring.

Four hours into the operation, Mr. Essien came to the control room with a gallon of naphtha. Yes! We've succeeded in producing gasoline.

Mr. Chijioke picked up the speaker.

"This is Refinery calling; come in His Excellence's office," he signaled.

"Go ahead, Refinery," the radio responded.

"Inform His Excellency that petrol is flowing at the refinery again," Mr. Chijioke said.

We began to celebrate with cheers, and as we were getting ready to go home, we heard the radio.

"His Excellency calling Refinery; come in Refinery," the head of state radioed.

"Your Excellency, command successfully executed," Mr. Chijioke said. "We've struck petrol, and the complex is fully functional; the

The Courage To Aspire

intelligence and expertise of Biafrans can no longer be questioned."

"Congratulations," he said. "I had no doubt that you would rise to the occasion. We are counting on you and your team. Tell everybody that I am proud of their accomplishment."

One week later, I received a pass and military protective rank. The pass allowed me to move or travel freely without obstruction or impediment, and it was stamped and signed by the head of state.

In the evening, more news broke: The federal forces had massed on the northern border of Biafra—moving south across the border to Nsuka. Odumegwu Ojukwu declared war to stop the federal forces' advance into Biafra. Therefore, the battle began, and we produced enough petrol every day to support war activities.

Suddenly, the federal forces captured the Island of Bonny, and jet bombers started to bomb the refinery—almost every day. Workers took cover as the warning system went off; we did not suffer any casualties. A few weeks later, we got radio news about the total collapse of the Nsuka sector.

One afternoon we heard that Biafran forces were advancing toward Ibadan. We cheered and celebrated. A few months later, we got another radio message indicating that the federal troops had beaten Biafran forces back toward Benin City; a day later the federal soldiers reached Asaba. Everything changed, and we became fearful and uncertain about the refinery.

One morning, on March 3, 1968, I went to the Okarika jetty to make visual inspections. When I got to the jetty, uncomfortable eerie and quietude had settled over the ever-busy sea port. I heard the sound of gunshots down the river, and Biafran soldiers were moving toward the river in their trucks.

Suddenly a plane bombed the refinery. The petrol tank exploded, and I joined the firefighters to put the fire out. I Forgot that the firefighters had protective gears on and I had none. Then another tank exploded, setting my pant and my legs on fire. Shortly, The Head of State's office ordered us to evacuate. The situation was chaotic.

Before leaving the refinery at Eleme, I stopped by Fortune's house so we could leave the imminent war zone together, but she wanted to see her mother before leaving. But the pain in my legs was excruciating, so I could not go with her. I got home and found the drugstore closed and no possibility of treating my burn. Therefore, I broke two eggs and rubbed the yolk—jellylike substance on my legs before joining the crowd running for safety.

Fortune and I left Port Harcourt headed in entirely different directions. She flew along Aba Road, and I went along Ikwere Road. I walked for more than thirty miles with my bad legs before the Red Cross picked us up and took us to Aba. For some inexplicable reason, Fortune and I arrived at the same spot and at the same time. On our arrival at the intersection of Asa and Azikiwe Roads, I was disembarking my truck, while she was getting off hers. She told me where she would be staying, and I gave her my relatives' address; then we parted company again. I was in too much pain to chat. I needed to go home and rest my legs.

Fortune and I visited each other a couple of times. Before she visited me, I told my uncles in advance, so when she visited, they received her warmly.

One week later, I reported at a primary school in Uzuakoli, where I received a big Honda model 250 motorcycle. Villagers had cleared a large area and leveled the ground.

On Sunday morning, the management staff had a meeting.

"Ndukwe, you will be going to Egbema with pipefitters, and you will be accompanied by a platoon of the Biafran forces," Mr. Chijioke said. "The area is a war zone. Your job is to bring back the electric generator from Shell BP oil field, and the pipe fitters will bring back as many pipes as possible. The soldiers will provide you with protection and tell you when to evacuate. You are leaving as early as the soldiers get here."

When we arrived at Egbema oil field, instead of tracing and disconnecting wires, I yanked switches and cables, unbolted the generator from the cement base, and threw everything into the truck. Then I helped the pipefitters to load the pipes into the truck. Suddenly, the soldiers gave us a signal to get in the truck. As we were leaving the oil field, the federal soldiers opened fire, but Biafran soldiers did not return fire.

Making a right turn at the main road, we could see the federal

The Courage To Aspire

soldiers moving toward us, probably in an attempt to cut us off.

When we came back, I designed the electrical system and drew the schematics, and the electricians went to work wiring and connecting machines and motors. We wired the primary school for refinery workers to stay in. In one week, we provided electrical power and light to the new refinery and its surrounding areas, which was sooner than we had expected. We completed the construction work and started producing petrol for Biafra again.

I visited my relatives a few times a week and gave some friends petrol. I had a quota of four gallons a week, but I used only one gallon, so I had to give away the remaining three gallons.

One afternoon, a girl accompanying an army officer gave me a letter from Fortune. She was staying in a refugee camp, and an army officer had beaten her, so she sent for me. I took off on my Honda 250 with my badge clearly displayed on my chest, but I was not wearing a military uniform, which was unfortunate. A few miles after Umuahia, a major stopped me at a checkpoint. He ignored my badge, stripped off my clothes, and ordered me to sit down with a group of young men who were waiting to join the training camp. I was getting ready to sit down when Brigadier Okongwu spotted me as his vehicle was crossing the checkpoint.

He stopped, got out, and walked toward me. I stood up and saluted him.

"Ndukwe!" he yelled.

"Yes, sir," I answered.

"Why are you here, and where are your machine and your badge?" he asked.

"Major took everything from me, sir," I answered.

"Major, get his clothes, his badge, and his machine," he ordered.

The officer brought everything back, and I got dressed. The brigadier pinned a green ribbon across the top of my badge and ordered the major into his van.

"Ndukwe, carry on," he said.

"Yes, sir," I responded.

He drove off with the major, and I hopped on my motorcycle and continued. When I got to the camp, I introduced myself to the officer in charge and declared my reason for coming to the military camp, as required.

"What's your function, officer?" the commanding officer asked.

"Providing the Biafran government with the petrol to prosecute the war, sir," I said.

"Oh, you are one of those," he said in a demeaning tone. He told somebody to call Fortune, and she came and showed me her wounds—from whiplashes. I was irate—but I could not say much in the military camp.

"Officer, why did my girlfriend receive such painful punishment?" I inquired.

"She violated the camp's code of conduct. She was caught stealing," he said.

I did not want to argue in his zone of authority, but I knew that Fortune would not steal anything. She would not even take money from me when I tried to give her some. She got on my machine, and we took off and rode back to Uzuakoli.

"I am sorry they did that to you," I said.

"Some girls conspired and misreported me," she said

"It's all right. You are safe now," I replied. She lived with me from that day until the end of the war.

One day we were on our way to Abariba to visit her mother where she was staying with Nnanna Kanu. We stopped at my village to greet Mom before continuing. Fortune was sitting on my motorcycle while we were chatting with Mom.

When I took off, she fell off the machine and landed on the exhaust pipe. She burned her leg and screamed in pain. I felt like dying right there. She got up, and Mom rubbed some oil on her leg. Then we continued on and visited her mother as planned.

Late in November 1968, I went home to visit Mom. On my way back, sounds of gunshots were coming from everywhere, not unlike the sound I had heard at the Refinery at Okarika Jetty before the refinery fell. When I got back to the refinery, an evacuation order was in effect, and electricians and pipefitters were disconnecting wires and pipes and loading everything on the military truck. I joined them and made sure the electrical generator was on the truck. Then I went back home to

The Courage To Aspire

evacuate Mom and Cathy, but they refused to go with me, so I came back and left Uzuakoli with Fortune.

I had received a message from my friend at the Barclays bank that they were settling at Añara Mbaise, so we went straight to Añara. A week later, I arrived at Amandugba Mbaise, where we built another refinery under tall trees in a thickly wooded area to cover up the refinery and prevent it from being bombed by the federal jets.

We operated the refinery there without the threat of bomb attack. One night, on January 14, 1970, I was getting ready to go home for the night when news came through our shortwave transceiver.

"Calling all sectors, come in all sectors. We have a truce; the war is over. Surrender to the federal forces; you are safe to do so," the radio announced.

I went home in disbelief. It was like a bad dream. The following morning, Fortune and I visited her mother at Mbieri; from there, the two of them got in a Red Cross truck and returned to Port Harcourt. Then I took another Red Cross truck and went home.

When I arrived home, I learned from Mama Ijeoma—who lived at the refugee camp in Obudu, with Mom—that she had died in the refugee camp as a Catholic priest was praying for her. Millions of people were killed during the war. The Muslim Hausa soldiers had captured Cathy, my brother Anyele died in the battle, and Dad and my brother Dick were safe. They took refuge in the bush—by the farmland. The following day, I told Dad I was traveling to Port Harcourt to check on Fortune and her mother.

It was impossible to predict their location because Port Harcourt is a big city. Her mother had lived in the Ports Authority housing quarters before the war. But new occupants were living there at the time.

Dad hesitated when I announced where I was going; Ibos were still facing persecution everywhere, and the danger was real.

"OK, you should not be afraid," he said. "You will go and come back safely. It is a good thing for a man to look for his wife in a situation like this."

Fortune and I had mutually agreed to get married after the war—with the approval of our parents.

I took off to Port Harcourt in a Red Cross truck. When I arrived at

Chuks I. Ndukwe

the Ports Authority and disembarked the truck, I saw the mob beating somebody to the ground. Strengthened by Dad's approval—and the belief that I was invisible to the crowd—I continued down Creek Road. Suddenly somebody grabbed me from behind.

"Uncle, Uncle, I am glad that you are safe. Come let me show you where sissy is," the voice said.

When he let me go, I turned around and saw Fortune's brother Sunny—or so I thought at the time. He took me to a house where Fortune and her mother hugged me.

"This is a miracle. How did you know where we are settled?" Fortune's mother asked.

"I had no idea. I was compelled to come and look for the two of you," I said.

"Compelled by who? Do you know how much you risked your life?" she asked.

"Dad said that it was safe for me to come. Nothing else mattered," I replied.

We visited Fortune's father the following day in Bonny. (He had not been living with Fortune's mother; they were not married). I spent two days with him, and before we returned to the city, I sought his consent to marry Fortune. The following day, Fortune's mother gave me some Nigerian currency then I went home to let Dad know I had found them, and they were safe.

Chapter 15
Fitting Reward

Life isn't supposed to be easy. Generally speaking, the harder something is the more rewarding the results will be.

~ C.C. Hunter

Two days after my return from Port Harcourt, I boarded a train to Enugu to register for resettlement at the secretariat as workers who lost their jobs during the war were being resettled within the eastern region. The train was full of Hausas traveling north; probably they were displaced by the Ibos returning to their homes or people going home for a visit or a combination of the two. They were restless and boisterous. The images and news of Ibos killed and maimed by these people were fresh in my mind, so I stayed frozen in my seat until the train stopped at the Enugu train station. Stepping on the platform, I saw Mr. Amaobi Anyanwu. He was the school prefect when I was attending GTC Enugu and had received a scholarship to study in Japan when I was a freshman. We had shared a dormitory then, and I was his dormitory aide.

"Ndukwe!" he screamed.

"Sir," I answered.

"Don't call me, sir; you are not a freshman at GTC anymore," he said.

"But it feels strange to call you Anyanwu," I replied.

"I'm glad to see you. We heard about you a lot during the war; you made us proud. Have you seen Nnyama?" he asked.

"No, I am just arriving, and you are the first person I've seen. How is he?" I asked.

"He's fine; he came home last week. Did you know Amandugba is close to our hometown?" he asked.

"No, I did not."

"Do you have a place to stay?"

"No, I do not."

"OK, I will take you to my uncle's house on Ogbete Road in Ogbete," he said.

When we arrived at Ogbete, the area had almost recovered from the destruction it suffered during the war. He introduced me to his uncle, who rented a room to me then he gave me some money, and told me he would come back to see me after I had completed the registration.

"Have you registered for resettlement yourself?" I asked.

"No, I don't need to. I was here before the war ended. I will tell you about it when I come back," Anyawu said.

The following day I went to Ogbete Market and bought pots and pans, other utensils, and a mat for sleeping. I also bought *gari*, *egusi*, crayfish, yams, plantain, oil, *oha*, salt, *egusi*, and pepper. Then I went home and cooked. Later in the afternoon, I went out again and bought writing pads and a pen.

On Monday, I went to the secretariat. I could not make my way anywhere close to the ministries; the line of people waiting for the interview was too long. I walked around the complex, trying to decide which ministry (department) to register with; I was thinking about the ministry in which officials were aware of my work during the war. I saw lots of people I knew, but I had forgotten their names, so I tried to avoid them.

"Hello! Ndukwe," a voice shouted

"Hello, I met Anyanwu on the train station platform yesterday and asked about you," I said.

"He was asking about you too," Nnyama said.

We walked around the complex together and met quite a few former GTC alumni. Then we decided to register with the Ministry of Education thinking they would post us to GTC or College of Technology for a good position, and from there we could get into the University of Nigeria. After trying for four days, I registered on Friday for an appointment for an interview and placement.

On Saturday, Anyanwu came by and took me out to dinner. After dinner, he showed me a new building in the independent layout—a location where government workers lived in Enugu and set aside to commemorate Nigeria independence from the United Kingdom.

The Courage To Aspire

"This building is going to be a hotel," Anyanwu said. "I am looking for somebody to design and supervise the electrical installation. I heard about your performance during the war, and I think you are the right person."

"That won't be a problem, but I can only work for you until I am resettled," I said.

"That's fine. I want you to do the design first and specify wire sizes, current-carrying capacities, and fuse types for each circuit so that the electricians can carry on when you leave," he said.

We walked through the entire building from the ground floor to the fifth floor.

"I would need a drawing table, the blueprint, the list of appliances you intend to install in each room, and the anticipated location of the bed for each room," I said.

He took me to one large room and showed me everything I was asking for. He also gave me money for two weeks because my appointment for the interview and placement was two weeks away. We did not discuss salary, but the money he gave me in advance was enough to start with as a temporary job. When I went home, I wrote letters to Fortune, Dad, and my brother Dick.

Dick joined me as soon as he got my letter. When he arrived in Enugu, I gave him money to start a secondhand clothing business. He went to Ogbete Market every day, and I went to work designing and supervising electrical wiring of Anyanwu's hotel.

One week later, Fortune joined us. After dinner on the day she arrived, we lay on the mat and chatted all night.

"I still can't believe you risked your life to come to Port Harcourt to look for me, and your father let you do that," she said.

"Dad was speechless when I told him, but it wasn't risky to me. I just wanted to know that you were safe," I said.

"What did you do?" Dick asked.

"I went to Port Harcourt to look for Fortune at the end of the war; Dad and I had kept it secret," I said.

"He told me that you went to visit a friend; you could have gotten killed," he said.

"You're right," Fortune said. "They killed lots of Ibos who were trying to return to their houses."

"I wasn't concerned about death after Dad approved of my wish to go," I said.

On Saturday, Fortune and I went out sightseeing. We walked around the East Regional Secretariat and the house of assembly; then we went to the Independent layout to see the hotel where I was supervising the electrical installation. Finally, we went to the Ogbete Market, where my brother was trying to make a fresh start. We looked for him all over the market until we found him by the main road where he was showing some women blouses and scarves.

When we went home in the evening, we cooked dinner and waited for my brother to come home before we ate.

"What happened to your mother and sister?" Fortune asked.

"Mom died at the refugee camp when a priest was praying for her," I said. "I was glad that she died in the hands of a priest. She had become very spiritual."

"What happened to your sister, Cathy? Did she survive?" she asked.

"Don't talk about her. The Hausa soldiers captured her and carried her away. Moreover, she was my brother Dick's wife-to-be. They didn't want her to know that."

In the evenings after dinner, we lay in the backyard and chatted about the first day we met and about the war, especially the day Port Harcourt fell into the hands of the federal forces.

"How did you know that Port Harcourt was going to fall that day?" she asked.

"I heard the sound of gunshots when I went to Okarika Jetty," I explained. "Then when I came back to the refinery, a plane bombed the complex and the oil tanks. Finally, the Head of the State's office ordered us to evacuate. We had a radio transceiver at the refinery, so we were updated regularly on the progress of the war." I did not tell her about my legs.

"You had an important position. I'm proud of you," Fortune said.

On the day of my interview and placement at the Ministry of Education, she wanted to go with me, but I discouraged her. I wasn't sure how long I would be there. I dressed up in my black suit and

The Courage To Aspire

carried the originals of all of my diplomas and certificates. When I arrived at the Ministry of Education, I waited outside until sometime after lunch.

Finally, the clerk called "Mr. Ogbuleke Ikebie Ndukwe."

"Right here," I answered.

"Please come with me," she said.

I followed her to the conference room and found familiar faces: Mr. Ahuchogu, my direct manager at the refineries; Mr. Mba, who had offered me a scholarship at GTC; and members of the petroleum management board during the war.

"Good afternoon sir," I said.

"Good afternoon," they replied.

I handed my credentials to Mr. Ahuchogu, and he had seen them during my interview at the refineries, so he passed them around.

Each one of them looked at me after going through my papers.

"His qualifications are much higher than that of the current principal of the GTC," Mr. Mba said.

"His qualifications are the same level as Mr. Njoku's, the electrical engineer at the refinery," Mr. Ahuchogu said. "That was the reason we did not place him directly under him. As you, all are aware; he did a spectacular engineering job at the refinery. He personally made it possible for us to restart the refinery operations after the British engineers disconnected the electrical system before they departed. Mr. Ndukwe put that system back together without supervision. We owe him our gratitude."

"Mr. Ndukwe's performance during the war was outstanding! We must thank him," Mr. Mba said.

They made copies of my papers and gave the originals back to me.

"You have been registered for placement, and we would like you to come back for our final decision. See the clerk for your appointment," Mr. Mba said.

I went to the clerk's office and received a new appointment to come back in two weeks. Then I went home and told Fortune about the interview.

"What did they ask you?" she asked.

"Nothing directly," I said.

Chuks I. Ndukwe

"That wasn't an interview," she said.

"Well, Mr. Ahuchogu and Mr. Mba were among the interviewers, and they know my capabilities and qualifications," I said

"The fact that Mr. Ahuchogu was among the interviewers, means you would definitely get a good position," she said.

When I went to work the next day, I informed Mr. Anyanwu about my new appointment for placement, and he was more than pleased to hear the news. So he paid me for two more weeks in advance, and he gave me money for one month rent. I gave Dick the money, which was enough for him to go back to Aba and resume his trading business. One week later, he left Enugu and went back to Aba.

I had paid my rent already, so I kept the rent money Anyanwu had given me. At that time, I had finished designing the electrical layout specifying wire routing, socket positions, junction boxes, the grounding points, and current-carrying capacities of all the wires and fuses. Before the day of my placement, electricians had run the wires and started to connect the cables to their specified termination points.

On Monday, I went to the Ministry of Education for my placement. I waited as people came out of the placement hall with sheets of paper instructing them where to go next. Suddenly, the clerk called my name.

"Mr. Ndukwe, you are next," she said.

When I entered the conference room, I greeted the officials and stood before them.

"Mr. Ndukwe, this committee has carefully reviewed your qualifications," Mr. Mba said. "We concluded that it would be a great service if you could impart your electrical engineering knowledge to the young students in this state, so we have decided to appoint you the vice principal at Ahiara Trade Center in Mbaise. On behalf of the committee members, I would like to congratulate you on your brilliant performance during the conflict. We're proud of you."

Thank you, sir," I said.

"Whenever you come to Enugu, please do stop by my office," Mr. Mba said. I stopped by the clerk's office and collected my placement brochure and went home.

When I got home, Fortune was waiting eagerly to hear the outcome of my visit to the ministry.

The Courage To Aspire

"How did it go?" she asked.

"Better than I expected," I said.

"So what did they say?"

"I am going to the Ahiara Trade Center as their vice principal."

"You are too young for that," she said.

"I don't think age has anything to do with it."

"How did they know that you are qualified?" She asked.

I simply gave her my papers and told her what each represented in the government's classifications.

"That's how they know," I said proudly.

"So, you actually knew what you were doing at the refinery?" she asked.

"Are you saying that you had doubts about what I was doing at the refinery?" I asked.

"Well, I wasn't sure, but you were very confident," she said.

On Monday, I escorted Fortune to the train station, from where she boarded the train back to Port Harcourt.

"I will see you again in Ahiara," she said before entering the train.

I stayed for a week to give Anyanwu the full account and progress report on the job I was doing for him. One day, we went through everything I had done, and since he was an electrical engineer himself, he was satisfied with the job I had done for him. So he took me out to dinner.

"During your freshman year at GTC, I could tell that things would turn out well for you; thank you for helping me," he said.

He dropped me off at home and gave me extra payment for one week.

"What's this for?" I asked.

"You can call it a bonus or a show of appreciation," he said.

"Thank you for your help," I replied.

Chapter 16
Giving Back

When life gives you lemons, chunk it right back.

~ Bill Watterson

On Friday, I left everything I had for Anyanwu's Uncle and boarded a train to Ovim. Then I took a Red Cross truck home to my village. At dinner, Dad asked about my trip to Enugu and whether I was going back to the refinery. Then he paused.

"I hope you are still going to marry that river girl," Dad said.

"Yes, she came to Enugu and spent two weeks with my brother and me," I replied.

"I know; Dick told me," he said.

When I arrived at Ahiara Trade Center, I was surprised to find out that the school did not have residences for instructors. However, somebody told me about a vacant room for rent, so I went there and rented the room. The landlord's wife escorted me to their market, and I bought everything I needed for cooking and then I went home and cooked.

The school began on Monday and my room was located right across from the southern end of the school. Looking at the school through my window, I could see students walking to school aimlessly and uninspired. It was not easy to differentiate between the students and the teachers. I waited until a black car arrived at the school and a motorcycle roared in too. Then I left my room and walked to school. Students gathered in groups yelling names and chatting loudly but disappointed their school—Saint Joseph's Trade School was renamed Ahiara Trade Center.

The principal rang the opening bell and disappointedly, the students learned that school would not start with devotional assembly and

The Courage To Aspire

prayers. Instead, students gathered in the field at the center of the classroom buildings.

"Good morning and welcome to Ahiara Trade Center," the principal said. "Returning students will go to their departments and clean up the classrooms and the workshops. Those of you seeking admission will fill out entrance-examination application forms. My office will let you know the date of the examination."

The principal, Peter Nwankwo, called a meeting of the staff in his office. When teachers met inside the principal's office, I handed my placement letter to him. He gave me a whimsical look with attitude, and then Gabriel Maduka—a fellow teacher—gave him his placement letter too. The principal stood up and looked around.

"The Ministry of Education has appointed Mr. Ndukwe the new vice-principal of Ahiara Trade Center," the principal said. "And we have a new member of the teaching staff; he graduated from the College of Technology Enugu."

The room fell silent for a few minutes. The returning teachers murmured among themselves and turned to glance at Gabriel and me. The school did not have offices for the teachers, nor did it have an office for the vice principal.

"The returning teachers will continue their functions. I will teach English language and mathematics in all classes, and Mr. Ndukwe will teach electrical principles, physics, and mathematics in junior and senior classes," he said. "Mr. Gabriel Maduka will teach mechanical engineering principles, mathematics, and physics in classes one through three. School supplies will be arriving within the week. Mr. Ndukwe will share an office with me—and he will deputize for me in my absence."

Workers had converted the woodwork-shed to a teachers' lounge. On Thursday a trailer truck arrived carrying school supplies, books, shelves, chairs, and tables for teachers. Two weeks later, the principal conducted the entrance examination. Three weeks later, he conducted interviews by himself and issued acceptance notices to successful candidates.

One day, the principal went to Enugu to attend a meeting. When he returned, he called a meeting to discuss matters that had come up during his trip to Enugu.

"The ministry has discovered that some people who were posted to some jobs did not actually have the qualifications they claimed to have during the registration and placement period," the principal said. "So the ministry will be conducting inspections in all schools to verify the qualifications of each teacher. I suggest that you keep your certificates and diplomas handy, so you don't get taken by surprise."

Teachers seemed happy to hear the announcement; they looked at each other and smiled. It did not take long before rumors began to fly around that Mr. Ndukwe would not last long at the school. Some predicted that Mr. Ndukwe and Gabriel Maduka would resign before the inspection officials arrived at the school for verification of teachers' qualifications.

Gabriel and I had become good friends. We rode around on his motorcycle. Sometimes we went to Umuahia, and some other times we went to Owerri just to ride around.

"I had one of these during the war," I said.

"What happened to it?" he asked.

"I left it at Amandugba Refinery," I said.

"Why didn't you take it home?" he asked. "We could have been riding together."

"The Hausa man would have taken it from me on my way home," I said.

***

Classes began with the principal kicking off mathematics for the senior class. I happened to be passing the classroom when he was talking, and the students were drowning his voice out. I peeped over the raised wall and saw that students were talking to each other instead of listening to Mr. Nwankwo.

After a while, he stormed out of the classroom. It was my turn to teach the next mathematics class. When I entered the classroom, I hit my staff on the table and yelled, "All stand! Sit. Stand. Good morning class, be seated."

"The war is over, and I am aware that some of you were officers in

The Courage To Aspire

the military, and you deserve my respect," I said. "I am not going to do any teaching today. Instead, we will get to know each other and our experiences during the conflict. You can tell us what you did and your rank and any juicy story you want to share. I can start if you like."

"Yeah! You can start," they shouted.

"I am from Alayi in Bende Division. I am a graduate of UAC Technical College in Sapele. I worked at the Nigerian Refineries in Eleme, Port Harcourt, before the war, I was responsible for getting the refinery restarted after white people had disconnected the system following an order to leave Biafra by Odumegwu Ojukwu. I built new electrical systems for new refineries during the war. I was specifically sent here to impart the knowledge that enabled me to do what I did during the war to students here at Ahiara Trade Center," I said. "I had a military protective rank of second lieutenant and a pass signed by Odumegwu Ojukwu authorizing me to move freely without impediment. I had a motorcycle—a Honda 250—I lost my mother and my brother too. I worked with soldiers, and I understand what you went through during the war. However, you must understand that the war is over, and you have to rebuild your future. This is my story; what is yours? Let's hear it; talk about sectors, camps, officers, or anything you like."

One student stood up and told a story about a battalion he lost in an ambush. "I was a major in command, and I have not slept well since then. This is the first time I am talking about it."

I asked everybody to come out and surround Emenike Uche. We surrounded him and hugged him.

"Emenike, you and your comrades fought to protect us; we are grateful and proud of you," I said.

"So, do you want me to teach you or not?" I asked.

There was silence for a few minutes until one student said, "Yes, sir." Then everybody followed.

"OK, this is the rule; you can call it the rule of engagement," I said. "When I step into the class, you will pay attention because I will not repeat myself. When I conduct an illustration on the board, each student will repeat what I did until everybody is comfortable with the material. You are free to correct me when I make a mistake. There is no penalty for doing so; instead, it will earn you credit," I said. "I will announce topics or lessons in advance, so you can read up and prepare for the class. Finally, you can come over to my residence and study with me or ask me questions or ask for help. You can eat whatever I have, but you must never leave my water container empty. Is that fair?"

"Yes, sir," everybody said.

Every student stood up and told the class his or her story, and a few more students revealed that they had been officers in the army. We had thirty minutes left before the beginning of the next class. I ran to the principal's office and returned with a soccer ball.

"Come on. Let's go to the field and release the tension in our bodies," I said.

We ran to the field and kicked the ball around, dribbling, attacking, and passing to whoever was available until the bell went off.

"Get ready for the next class; we will get down to work," I said.

I went to classes with my staff and no books. Other teachers went to classes carrying textbooks, but when I entered the class I took control by yelling, "All stand sit, stand, and be seated. Who's not here?" Before the roll call.

"If you have your textbook, open page—(.….Our lesson today is—…) If you don't have your textbook, pay attention, and take notes."

I'd make my introduction, discussed the material, and carefully explained the derivation of equations when applicable. We solved problems on the board until every student understood each step. Some days we stayed after classes until they understood the process and could go through it individually. My room was crowded every evening with seniors studying while I prepared materials for my lessons. On weekends they came over and studied until they fell asleep or got tired or hungry. Shortly, my room became a comfortable place for them to relax and study. Occasionally, I left them in my room and went over to Gabriel's house.

One day the principal followed me to my mathematics class.

"All stand. Be seated," I said, and the class was quiet.

"Mr. Ndukwe, can I see you?" He asked.

"Yes, what is it?" I asked.

"How did you get these monsters of students to behave?" he asked.

The Courage To Aspire

"They are not what you think of them," I said. "The students are young men who'd just returned from the war theater."

He sat down and watched me throughout the class period. Three months later, the Ministry of Education inspectors arrived unexpectedly. They met with the principal briefly and came over to my class just as I was entering the classroom.

"All stand; be seated," I said.

The class was quiet. I introduced the lesson the usual way and discussed the material. As I was writing on the board, one student stood up. "Sir, you missed something," he said.

"Ikenga, would you go to the board and correct the mistake?" I asked.

He went to the board and corrected my mistake.

"Thank you, I am glad that you are paying attention. Now let's explore how this equation was derived in the first place," I said.

The inspectors left the class and went to the principal's office. The team comprised of Mr. William Eke, the Mbaise divisional education officer; Mr. Mba, the regional educational inspector; and four other officials. Shortly after leaving my classroom, they sent for me. When I entered the principal's office, they had copies of my certificates and diplomas on top of a pile of files.

"Mr. Ndukwe, how do you like your new job?" Mr. Mba asked.

"I am enjoying it," I said.

"Your students seem to be under control, unlike at other schools where students are unruly and out of control," he said.

"They were that way at the beginning, but I worked on it for a week. Now we trust each other, and they are happy to learn," I said.

"It was clearly evident watching you and the students in the class," Mr. Mba said.

"We don't have any questions for you. We have your papers. The ministry has increased your salary to reflect your highest certificate, and your position of a vice-principal is permanent. Congratulations," Mr. William Eke said and shook my hand.

"Stay and help us. Call the next person on the list," Mr. Mba said.

I called other teachers to the principal's office for conversations with the inspectors. Some teachers had lost their certificates during the war; others produced their certificates, and the inspectors adjusted their salaries accordingly. After the inspection, the principal, and I escorted the inspectors to their car, then we chatted for a while before they left the school.

"What did they tell you?" Maduka asked.

"They raised my salary and made my position permanent," I replied.

"They raised my salary too," he said

We took off on his motorcycle, went to Owerri, and relaxed in one of the bars for a while and enjoyed orange juice. Miss Edina had become Gabriel's girlfriend, so he told her what had happened during the inspection, and Miss Edina spread the news that I was a permanent vice-principal of the school.

At that time, I had ordered past question papers for electrical installation examinations from the City and Guilds of London Institute. When the documents arrived, I used them as my teaching materials.

Feeling confident that the students were fully ready for the examination, I ordered application forms and encouraged them to apply for the exam. In June, they applied for the test, which they took in our school. In September. When the results came out, all the students passed. It was the first time students from that school graduated with a technical certificate. I was gratified that I lived up to the expectations of the ministry officials that sent me there.

✳✳✳

One day I went to Maduka's house for dinner. He had received the Boston Globe newspaper in the mail earlier in the afternoon. His brother-in-law was a professor at MIT in Boston, so he sent him the Boston Globe every week. I opened one page and read something about a scientific machine—a computer that would behave like a human being; it would be able to read, write, and solve mathematical problems and a whole lot of other things. Two companies, one by the name Honeywell and the other IBM, were recruiting students to learn the art of programming the machines. At the end of the article, I saw an advertisement by the Honeywell Institute of Computer Science in

The Courage To Aspire

Burlington, Massachusetts. The school was recruiting students to its newly founded institution. I got excited, and I remembered the first time I had had that feeling of excitement; it was when the American scientists had demonstrated electric light in my primary school class. Therefore, I applied. And Maduka applied to Northeastern University for mechanical engineering.

A few weeks later, both of us received letters of acceptance. Maduka went to the American Embassy in Lagos for a visa, but the embassy rejected his visa application. I submitted my visa application through the Ministry of Education in Enugu.

When I went for an interview at the ministry, they did not know anything about computers, so I had to explain what I knew about this revolutionary scientific machine.

"You have a secure position in this ministry, but if you decide to pursue higher education, we will not stop you," they told me.

"I want to pursue higher education," I said.

"We will prepare a file for you to take to the American Embassy in Lagos for your visa interview. We will notify you when your file is ready," they said, "and we will make the appointment for your visit to the embassy."

I waited for the letter from the ministry for my appointment to the American Embassy in Lagos until I got discouraged, tired, and almost gave up hope. Meanwhile, Maduka had left Nigeria and tried to sneak into the United States through Canada. The immigration department sent him back.

One day, I was going to the bank to deposit my salary in Umuahia. As I was crossing a railroad track, I saw an elderly woman limping toward the train track. Then I rushed over and helped her pass the rail.

"Come with me, son; let me show you something," she said.

I helped her into the bar across the road.

"Sit down," she said.

"Let me buy something, so they won't throw us out," I said.

"Don't worry; they won't. You are getting ready to go to America, right?" she asked.

"Yes, ma'am," I answered.

"Somebody in the government is holding your file; he doesn't want you to go," she said. "I want you to go with that girl you want to marry to the seaside and turn your back to the sea. I want both of you to hold one piece of stone and throw it over your heads into the water together. Then your brother will take you to a place near your school in Mbaise. An old woman there will tell you about your journey; it will be rough, but in the end, it will be joyful. Good luck, my son."

When we came out of the bar, I turned around to take her hand, she was gone. I did not know what happened to her: she was not a ghost because she spoke clearly. She could not be a spirit because I touched her, and she spoke like a human. I temporarily went into a state of confusion and disbelief. I went to the bank and made my deposit, and then I went home. It took me days to accept what the old lady had said.

On Saturday, I traveled to Port Harcourt just as Fortune was arriving home from school. (She lived in the campus far from home). I told her the incredible story.

"Let's go and do it now," she said without any hesitation.

We went down to Creek Road and threw the stone in the ocean as the old lady had said. Then on my way home, I stopped in Aba and told my brother what the old lady had told me.

"That is strange. I don't know anybody from Ahiara, but I will find out," he said.

The following Saturday, I went back to Aba to see Dick.

"Somebody told me where to go. Come back on Friday. We will go on Saturday, so I can come back on Sunday," he said.

On Friday, I went to Aba again, then Dick and I went to Ahiara Mbaise and met with the other old lady. She repeated what the first old lady had told me in Umuahia. She gave me two signs.

"You will definitely have a dream tonight. If you see a paved road lined with light and flowers in your dream, you will be on your way to America shortly," she said, "but if you see an unpaved road, then your chance of traveling is zero."

After the meeting, we went home to my one-room residence; it was not far from the old lady's house. My brother laughed and laughed.

"I can't believe that a vice-principal of a college is living in one room; some vice principals live in a mansion," he said.

"This was the only vacant room I could find when I arrived here," I

The Courage To Aspire

said.

"Don't get me wrong," he said. "It's just the way you are. You don't see yourself as important; you are like a little boy all the time, no matter where you are."

I did not really appreciate what he said. In fact, I was offended. "Why did you say that?" I asked.

That was a rare occasion when we talked to each other seriously as equals. Usually, Dick would tell me what to do, and I would do it without hesitation.

"Do you remember when Star Breweries gave you a house in the European Quarters?" he asked. "You said no because you were too young to live there, and you wanted to live near Uncle Emeke Chima."

"Yes, I remember, but I wasn't acting like a little boy. I did not want to live there with a housemaid. I wanted to be near my uncle," I said.

"OK, but you lived in Milverton Avenue, and it wasn't near your uncle."

"True, but I could walk to Uncle Emeke's house any time," I said.

I cooked yam and stew because I did not feel like cooking soup and foo-foo after what he had said. After dinner, we played checkers, and he beat the hell out of me. He was that good at it.

When I went to sleep, I had a dream, and surprisingly, I saw one of the signs the old lady had told me to expect. It was, indeed, a spectacular sight. I did not tell my brother. I was afraid of telling anybody for fear that could alter the outcome; it was like a sacred vision. My brother went home the next day.

Two weeks later, the ministry invited me to Enugu and told me to be prepared to travel to Lagos from there. So I went to Aba and told my brother the letter had arrived. Then I traveled to Port Harcourt to tell Fortune then she decided that she was coming to Ahiara Mbaise for a visit, so I waited for her visit before going to Enugu for my interview with the ministry of education officials.

On the day of Fortune's visit, I waited all day until five o'clock in the evening. She usually arrived at about two o'clock when she had visited in the past. I panicked and gave my landlady, Mrs. Ngozi Ozuribe, the key to my room, and then I took off for Port Harcourt.

"Let's wait till tomorrow; she might be running late," she said.

"I have to go; something was bothering her, and I have to hear it," I said.

I arrived at her mother's house and found her room padlocked.

"Fortune is on her way to Mbaise," her mother said.

"OK, bye," I said, turned around, and went to the motor park.

When I got to the motor park, there was a taxi bound for Owerri that was looking for only one passenger. Before long, I was in Owerri. Then I took a kaikai bus to Ahiara. When I got home, I knocked on the front door. The landlord, Mr. Ozuribe, came out with a gun.

"Oh, Mr. Ndukwe, it's you," he said.

"Yes sir," I said as I pushed him aside and went inside the house.

Fortune and my landlady were in my room, chatting.

"Oh, goodness, he's back," Mrs. Ozuribe, shouted. "How did you manage to come back so fast?" she asked.

"I don't know; it happened too fast," I answered.

"Why didn't you stay in Port Harcourt till the next day?" Fortune asked.

"I didn't want to keep you worrying about me," I said. I hugged Fortune, and both of us fell on the bed.

"Wait till I leave the room before you start," Mrs. Ozuribe said humorously.

"OK, let me cook something for you. How was your trip?" I asked Fortune.

"Good. How was yours? Did you see my mother or Sunny?" she asked.

"Yes, I saw both, but I couldn't talk to anybody," I said.

"I cooked already. Take a bath while I set up the table," she said.

After the meal, we spent all night talking.

"I had to talk to you because I can't take it anymore. I have failed the West African Examination Council exams two years in a row, and my parents are calling me all kinds of names. I don't want to go back to school," she said sobbing.

I wiped her tears off and hugged her very tightly. I remembered the two nurses who had nursed me when I was a patient in the infirmary ward at Enugu General Hospital. They had not finished high school.

The Courage To Aspire

Auntie Lucy had not completed high school either.

"Look at me. You are not stupid. You will be all right," I said.

"How can you say that? I don't want to go back to school."

"First, as my wife, you will be all right. Second, your parents will look at you in the future and regret everything they are saying about you now," I said.

"Are you a magician?" she asked.

"If I don't succeed in going to America, at least I have a solid position in the Ministry of Education. You can be the wife of a vice principal," I said jokingly.

"Vice principal in one room?" she asked.

"This one-room occupant is very well paid; the money is in the bank," I boasted. "OK—joke aside—go to the general hospital and apply for nursing training school; high-school graduates and seniors are eligible."

She stood up and stared at me for a while before she left the room. When she came back, she kept staring at me.

"You had just graduated from college when I met you. I mean, you do not have a whole lot of experience in life," she said. "How do you know what to say at any time? My father is a graduate, and he does not think like you. Who are you?"

"Just go home and do what I suggested; we will face this world together. Do not ask me any more questions. I am tired of chasing you around." I gave her a light punch on the stomach.

"Are you trying to kill our babies inside my stomach?" she asked as she punched me back everywhere—mostly on my back.

"Good night," I said and lay down.

The next morning, we took a taxi to Owerri. Then she took a cab to Aba, and I took a bus to Enugu. When I arrived in Enugu, the ministry had made my flight reservation for December 9, 1972. They gave me the confirmation paper and put it in my file.

"Should the consul ask for your flight date, it is the date on the flight confirmation," the clerk said.

I went to Lagos, arriving on Friday in the evening. On Saturday, I went to the store at Udumota Square with Uncle Anyaele Ochu. Throughout the day, Yoruba women packed the store, buying all kinds of fabrics for curtains, for blouses, and mostly for their traditional attire. At the end of the day, I was exhausted from holding and folding the textiles while Uncle Anyaele Ochu cut the length requested by the customer. The weather was hot and humid, so I did not sleep comfortably.

Before leaving Ahiara, I had saved enough money to pay my tuition fees for one semester, so on Monday, Uncle Anyaele took me to the bank, and I wired the money to Honeywell Institute of Computer Sciences in Burlington, Massachusetts.

Arrived at the American Embassy very early in the morning on Tuesday, the embassy was filled with applicants looking for visas. When the consul called my name, my knees began to shake as I walked to the consul's counter and handed my file over to him.

The American consul looked at every paper in my file.

"What are your name and your date of birth?" he asked.

"What is your occupation, or are you a student?" he asked.

"What is a computer?" he asked.

I explained what I had read in the paper.

"If it is that new, as you said, how can you apply your knowledge when you return to Nigeria, or do you intend to remain in America after your graduation?" he asked.

"If indeed a computer is capable of solving mathematical problems and doing bookkeeping," I said, "banks, government offices, and commercial establishments will find its application useful, and I will be one of the pioneers to run it."

"Are you aware that your school started a week ago?" he asked.

"I would have left if the Ministry of Education had sent my invitation for an interview in time, but I will study hard to catch up if you grant me a visa," I said.

"Congratulations. Before you leave, you must do your vaccination and mail a money order for 150 Naira to the Ministry of Education in Enugu and bring a copy to this office," he said "It should have been the first thing they did. Good luck."

When I went back to the store, Uncle Anyaele took me to the bank. I did not have any more money to pay for the money order, so he paid for it and made a copy of it in the bank.

The Courage To Aspire

I mailed the stub to Enugu, and then I went back to the embassy. I did not feel like waiting in line again after waiting half of the day before for my interview, so I walked straight to the consul's window and slipped the copy of the money order with the request to do so in his window. He nodded and waved. I went back to the store, restless and overwhelmed by happiness.

Assisting relatives in the store became difficult; I was dropping things—especially textiles—when they asked me to hold one end as they cut off a piece. I dropped the whole thing several times; I was really shaking. They bought food and asked me to sit down and eat. They thought I was hungry, but it was not hunger. I was suffering from disbelief syndrome, which would take a good night's sleep to overcome.

On Monday, I left Lagos and went back to Aba. When I arrived, Fortune was waiting for me. She looked impatient, as though she had something on her mind.

"We have to get married before you leave," she demanded.

"No, we have to wait till you join me in America," I replied.

"We have to do it now," she insisted. "My friends told me that when men get to America; they fall in love with American girls. You will forget me when you get to America."

I was strongly opposed to the idea because Uncle Eke Anyaele Ochu had gotten married before he went to the United Kingdom, and his wife got pregnant after he left.

I remembered I had told Fortune she would be all right with me as her husband, so I complied. I had only seven days left before traveling, so I did not have enough time to post banns in the church. Instead, I went to the governor's office in Enugu and obtained permission for a civil wedding.

On the day Fortune and I got married, December 5, 1972, her family arrived from Port Harcourt early in the morning; my family gave them short, warm reception. Fortune was dressed in a beautiful white bridal gown, and I had my black suit on. After the reception party, both families went to Aba City Hall, where the city clerk conducted the marriage and issued us our marriage certificate. It was a hectic time for me, as I was busy making travel arrangements.

Chuks I. Ndukwe

Later in the evening, we had our reception in a large hall with many invitees in attendance. On Saturday, we traveled to my hometown, Alayi arriving in the afternoon. In the evening, my parents gave us a dinner party before we went to bed. On Sunday, my town held a send-off-party for me; people donated lots of money, which I left for my brother, and I departed that evening.

On Monday, I left Aba for Lagos with Fortune. When we got to Lagos, Uncle Anyele took me to the KLM office to get my plane ticket. The following day, I chatted with Fortune at the airport and said these words:

"You know that society does not treat women kindly when they have a baby outside marriage," I said "so you must protect yourself from such an unwanted and unplanned accidental pregnancy as I've been doing. But if it happens, you should not worry." Then we hugged and said good-bye. I boarded the bus to the tarmac to board the plane. Then I waved, and she waved back.

Now I boarded the plane and sat down, and passengers began walking up and down the aisle colliding with each other—as they tried to put their carry-on luggage in the overhead bin. I thought about the days gone by—how I fell in love with America when I was attending high-school social events at the American consulate in Enugu, including celebrating July 4 and partying with workers there. I remembered my meeting with the ministry of education officials—people I held in high regard when I was a student at GTC—how they praised me for my work during the Nigerian-Biafra war and posted me to Ahiara Trade Center as the vice principal of that school.

I thought about the mysterious old lady I had helped cross the railroad track in Umuahia and what she said about my journey to America. I wished Mom were alive. I thought about how she had sat directly opposite me and looked squarely into my eyes and talked about the virtues of decent living—rooted in the purity of heart, mind, and soul. I wondered what more she would have said. "May her soul rest in peace," I thought.

I wished my teacher Mr. Madubike Okocha and his wife, Helen, were around to give me advice. Finally, I recall the American scientist, Mr. David Marshal, who called me out in front of my class to turn on

The Courage To Aspire

electrical light. And I thanked God for sending him.

As the plane began to taxi to the takeoff point, my faith and belief in the infinite goodness and mercy of God—even for the undeserving like me—grew stronger.

Epilogue

Memories warm you up from the inside. But they also tear you apart.

~ Haruki Murakami

Just finishing the last sentence of this narrative, I began to think about the good O' growing-up days. I remembered that Saturday morning when the priest asked me to choose a baptismal name, and without hesitation, I chose Chukudi or Chuks [I believe in God]. And then I realized that was the most significant moment of my young life—the day I professed my solemn belief in God—and made this professing—my name.

Therefore, it should not come as a surprise that at thirteen, faith and spirituality had become a part of my thinking. Because—at a much younger age, I had watched Mom grieve to near-death when she lost her only daughter and became the spiritual mother of Christ Apostolic Church afterwards. I remember the day I jumped up in the class and shouted, "I want to become an electrical engineer—when I grew up." I had thought that my young spirit had glided away from that classroom like a bird to ask God to grant my wish. So this professing was nothing short of my innocent thinking that would become a significant part of my foundation and my comfort zone. This is not to say that I wanted to become a priest.

For me, though, gaining admission to the government trade center and scholarship to UAC technical college at Sapele put me squarely on my path to becoming an electrical engineer. I studied electrical principles; took part in experiments in the laboratory. Still, I kept thinking about the day I would light up a dark classroom with electric light.

Reading this narrative, I find it difficult to believe that despite the insurmountable financial and economic odds, I made it through technical college—directly out of the love and kindness of my school

The Courage To Aspire

teachers, Mr. and Mrs. Madubike Okocha—who welcomed me to their family for reasons I would never know.

Without a doubt, their support encouraged me to aspire to realize my wish. However, I must say, the couple did more than that—the couple instilled in me that incredible love of children most teachers share. Therefore, when I became a teacher, I looked at every student through the lens of my teacher's eyes and extended that same kindness and welcoming spirit to all of them.

My joy as a teacher came from three separate reasons: first, the way students would trip me up and pile up on me—when we played soccer in the field and came over to my house to cook and eat afterwards. Second, the students found my room their place of comfort, relaxation, and for studying after school. Third, the way they respected me in the classroom and paid attention to me while I was teaching, whereas other teachers found it difficult to control those same students.

I would be lying if I said that starting my professional life, as a supervisor after graduating from the technical college did not give me a sense of pride. And the recognition of my performance during the Nigeria-Biafra war by the government officials for designing, building, and supervising the electrical systems when foreigners had left Biafra was not intoxicating. After all, I chose UAC technical college because of the technical expertise I knew I would gain from the college.

Therefore, when the head of state ordered foreigners to leave Biafra, and they disabled the electrical system at the Nigerian refinery before leaving, I knew I would have some influence on the public debate and opinion on the Nigerian engineers and the technicians' ability to do the job the white man did exclusively in the past. I thought I would have something to say and do about that, and I did beyond my expectations.

Still I remained obedient to the culture that valued respect of the older people over one's technical ability. I did my job with humility—serving and running errands for the men, I supervised because I was younger than they were. Yet, they did everything I asked them to do.

In many ways, that culture of humility, obedience, and mutual respect served me so well and got me ready for the job of a manager in a much-advanced environment—high tech industry in the United States of America I never foresaw.

By all account, though, I can say that my short young life in Nigeria was exciting—that things worked out well for me. I look back now, and I cannot think of any dull moment. I participated in the events carried by the Nigerian Broadcasting Corporation—radio station in Enugu and appeared in debates organized by the Nigerian American friendship league and televised by the NBC television studios.

Also, I made few friends and thinking about the people I chose as friends and how successful all of them had become—without any black spot on their reputations, I pat myself on the back for having made good choices.

Not everything worked out, though, I could not sing in the choir nor play soccer I loved after suffering breathing impairment. I also regret that I was not able to work for the company that offered me a scholarship (Star Breweries) due to petty jealousy of one employee who thought that I was too young to be his boss. Without a doubt, I had hoped to work for the company and prove that the money they spent to educate me was worth the investment.

Most of all, and always fresh on my mind is my childhood wish to become an electrical engineer. And how happy I would be to light up a dark classroom—with electric light like the American scientist, Mr. David Marshal, who came to my class once and lit up my classroom with electric light.

Then like an act of God, I arrived at Uzuakoli Methodist School during the Nigeria-Biafra war, not knowing that my wish to light up a dark classroom was about to come true. We were there to build a new refinery—at a place where there was no electrical power and workers stayed in darkness. I remember arriving there, going to Egbema—Shell oil-field to bring back an electric generator. Shortly after returning from Egbema, I designed the electrical layout and wiring diagram that the electricians used to wire the new refinery and its surroundings, including the classrooms—where the workers stayed in darkness.

That was the highlight of my work during the war. On that day, and at that moment when the wiring of the classroom was completed, I could not help but remember my teacher and realized that my wish was

The Courage To Aspire

about to become a reality. Holding the switch, I paused, and workers wondered what I was waiting for. Finally, I turned the switch on, the classroom lit up, and workers cheered. Then I turned around, got on my motorcycle, and rode away.

Acknowledgements

I thank my late mother, Nwakego Ikebie Ndukwe, a quiet and soft-spoken woman, who taught me that every curious incident happens for a reason. "When that reason is not obvious, search for it," she said. I thank my late father, Ikebie Ndukwe, who taught me that a man without character, belief, or principle is one without footprints in the sand of time; the world forgets him soon after his departure.

I thank my late uncle, Emeke Chima, who gave me *Up from Slavery* by Booker T. Washington before I learned to read. I thank my late uncle, Okereke Chima, who gave me a bow and arrow and encouraged me to aim high in the sky and shoot beyond the clouds. I thank Alayi Methodist Central School's headmaster, Mr. Madubike Okocha, who saw my burning desire to become an electrical engineer and made it possible.

I want to express my sincere appreciation to my editors, Susan, and DJ for the job they have done in making this narrative come alive.

Glossary of Igbo Words

abaa
Black fruit—with the kernel that turns yellow when it is ripe for eating.

agwu
Shrine—used by Dibia to offer sacrifice to Chukwuobioma.

akara
Fried balls of dough of black-eyed peas.

akamu
A creamy blend of corn flour.

aku
Of the Orthopteran order of edible insects—like grasshoppers and locust. Their swarming flight causes them to collide and fall in large numbers when they invade the village. It's considered a delicacy.

Chukwuobioma
God of mercy.

compound
Space in the neighborhood surrounded by row houses—homes of related families.

dibia
Inducted member of the native herbal-medicine practitioners—one ordained to preside over ceremonies and sacrifices to the god of mercy.

egusi
Ground melon seed.

Eke
Farmers' market day observed by villagers as a holiday. One of the eight markets—located around eight different villages.

foo-foo
A dough of pounded cassava flour.

gari
A dough of grated fried casava

grass-cutter
Of the rodent order of Mammalia—like a porcupine, found in West Africa.

kaikai-bus
Old mini-bus

Igwu
Name of a local stream.

lorry
A large vehicle with wooden housing used for transporting heavy load and people.

maimai
Steamed wrap of dough of beans

mpataka
Fresh, thin slices of cassava—soaked in clean water for a minimum of four days.

nsi
A superstitious object believed to have the power to inflict pain.

nzu
A slab of chalk natives offers visitors as a welcoming symbol.

Ochufu
The alternative name of the village of Amigwu, Amankalu Alayi.

ofo'h
Idolized god of justice.

oha
Leaf of a nonfarm plant used by villagers to make soup—usually planted at backyards.

osoji
Spicy seed used by natives and *Dibias* to ward off evil spirit.

ukpo'h
Yellow groundnut used for making soup

urua
Soft, edible clay dug up from the waterside.

About The Author

Chuks I. Ndukwe, once a sought after engineer in the High Tech industry worked for such companies as the Codex Corporation, USRobotics, ADC Telecom, and Lucent Technologies mentoring junior engineers and managed research and development departments.

During his career, Ndukwe demonstrated strong strategic management skills. His problem-solving skills earned him "Key Contributor Award" at ADC Telecom, Minnetonka Minnesota. He built a strong team of engineers that performed above expectations—designing such technologies as caller identification, modems, routers, and Internet gateways.

Ndukwe is now retired and lives in Newark, New Jersey where he devotes his time writing to inspire others.

www.ingramcontent.com/pod-product-compliance
Lightning Source LLC
Chambersburg PA
CBHW070550010526
44118CB00012B/1280